195

# A Very Young Rider

Also by Jill Krementz

The Face of South Vietnam
(with text by Dean Brelis)

Sweet Pea—A Black Girl
Growing up in the Rural South

Words and Their Masters
(with text by Israel Shenker)

A Very Young Dancer

# A Very Young Rider

Written and Photographed by

*Jill Krementz*

Alfred A. Knopf.
New York, 1977

This is a Borzoi Book
published by Alfred A. Knopf, Inc.
Copyright © 1977 by Jill Krementz
All rights reserved under International and Pan-American Copyright Conventions.
Published in the United States by Alfred A. Knopf, Inc., New York, and
simultaneously in Canada by Random House of Canada Limited, Toronto.
Distributed by Random House, Inc., New York.

Library of Congress Cataloging in Publication Data

Krementz, Jill.
A very young rider.

1. Show riding—Juvenile literature.
2. Horses—Juvenile literature.
(1. Show riding. 2. Horses)
I. Title.
SF294.7.K73      798'.23      77-74996
ISBN 0-394-41092-0

Published October 18, 1977
Second Printing, October 1977

Manufactured in the United States of America

Graphics were directed by R. D. Scudellari; book design and
layout by Elissa Ichiyasu.

*For my parents,*
*Virginia and Walter Krementz,*
——————*with love*——————

I don't know if I'll ever make the United States Equestrian Team when I grow up, but I really want to. I started riding when I was three. I'm ten now. My name is Vivi Malloy. My pony's name is Ready Penny. She's a chestnut and I've had her for two years. I ride her in horse shows in the medium pony hunter division.

She's 13.1 hands high. A hand is four inches, and you measure a horse from the ground to its withers. That's the place at the base of the neck where the mane starts. A large pony can be as tall as 14.2 hands. After that it's a horse and you can't show it in pony classes.

My older sister Debby has two horses. She's seventeen and she's ridden in the Maclay Finals in Madison Square Garden for the past three years. That's the big junior equitation class over fences. She's hoping to qualify again this year.

My brother Mark is thirteen and he rides in quite a few shows too. All three of us are very active in the Pony Club. The Pony Club is a nationwide organization that runs all kinds of instructional and competitive activities for children seventeen and under and their ponies. It's really fun.

Mom used to ride a lot when she was my age and she still goes fox hunting. Most of the time she helps Debby, Mark, and me with our riding.

The nonriders in the family are Dad and my other brothers, Andrew and Kenneth. They like football, golf, skiing, and swimming much more than horses. Sometimes they come and watch us when we're in horse shows, but that's mainly because Mom talks them into it.

I wish I could ride all the time, but of course I have to go to school during the day. My favorite subject is math.

The first thing I do when I get home is to run and say hello to Penny. She's usually outside in the paddock if it's warm. When it's cold, she stays in her stall.

As soon as we're finished saying hello, I go back to the barn and muck out her stall. Mucking out is a daily chore, like making your bed. Penny's bed has to be warm and dry or she'll get thrush, which is a very bad foot disease. I have to take out the manure with a pitchfork and remove the wet bedding. Then I turn over all the bedding and smooth it down. After the stall is clean, I go back to the paddock and get Penny.

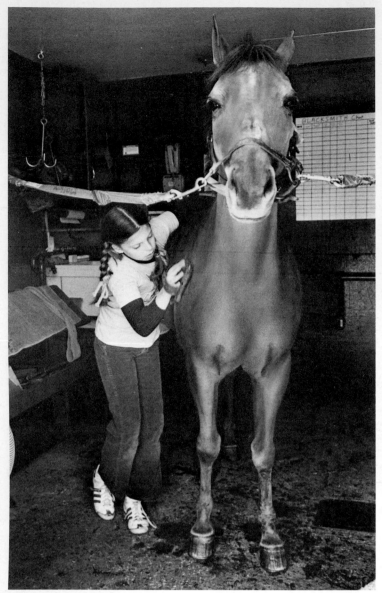 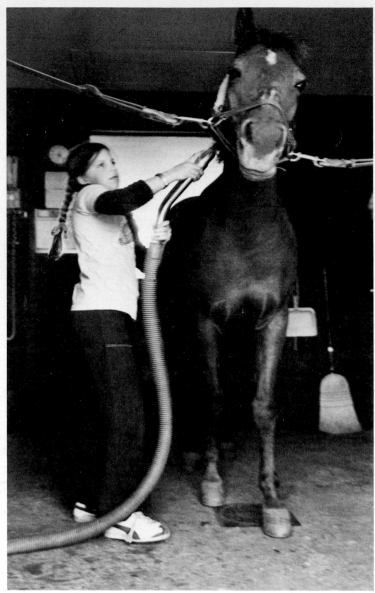

I bring her into the barn and put her on cross-ties. Then I start grooming her. First I use the curry comb to loosen the dirt and the long hairs on her coat. Then I vacuum her all over. This must tickle because Penny always flicks her ears when I do it.

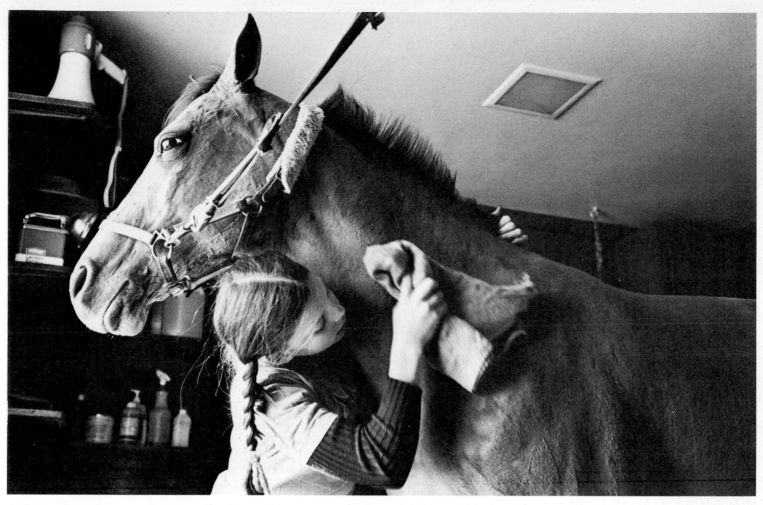

After that I use the body brush to get all her hair to lie flat and be shiny. Next step is to go all over her with a rub rag. Then I use the hoof pick because there could be some little stones stuck in her hoofs and that's bad. Last of all I treat her hoofs to keep them from getting dry and cracking. All this grooming takes about thirty minutes.

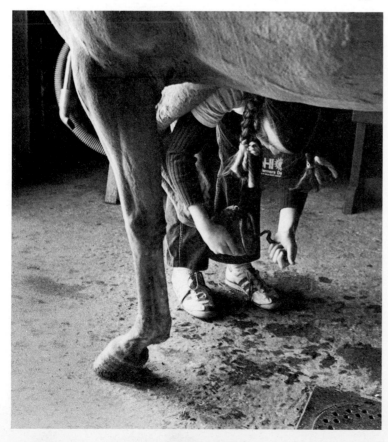
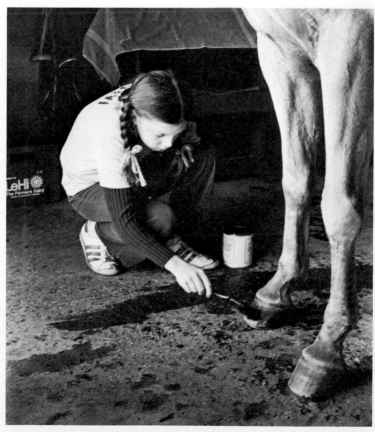

Then I put on my riding helmet, boots, and chaps. It's really dangerous to ride with sneakers because your foot can slide all the way through the stirrup and your ankle can get caught in the stirrup iron. The heel of a boot prevents this. The boots also protect your toes in case a horse steps on you. But not much.

After I'm dressed, I tack up Penny. She doesn't mind when I put the bridle on, but she doesn't like it when I tighten her girth. The girth is a leather strap that goes around her stomach and keeps the saddle on firmly. If it's not snug, the saddle slips.

Mom usually gives me a leg up. You always mount from the left because in medieval times knights wore their swords on their left side.

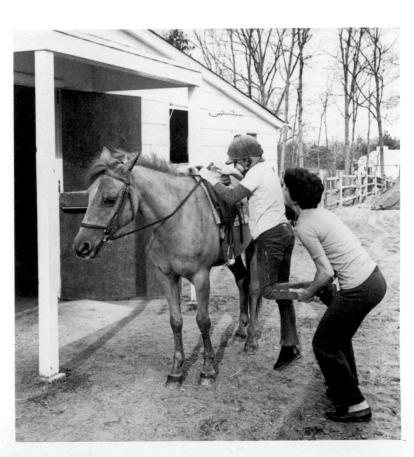

Behind the barn there's a riding ring. I ride for about an hour and practice my equitation, which means horsemanship. Good equitation is riding in the right position—your form, your style, and the way you fit your pony. It's very hard for me to keep my heels down so I work on that.

I show in the pony hunter division, which means that it's Penny's way of moving that's being judged, and not my equitation, but if my equitation isn't good, she won't look good either. Sometimes I ride in equitation classes so I won't get rusty.

What I try to work on is lightening my hands and sitting properly. People with heavy hands pull on the reins and that's very hard on a horse's mouth. Good hands are important because it's your hands that guide your horse.

I like jumping the best and so does Penny.

About once a week I have a lesson with Jonathan Devine. He works as an assistant for George Morris, who is Debby's trainer. George is really famous and all the best riders train with him. He used to be on the United States Equestrian Team, which represents the United States at the Olympics. He rode with the jumping team which won the Silver Medal in the 1960 Olympics in Rome. He doesn't train ponies though, so I'll have to wait until I'm older and bigger before I can train with him. But I really like training with Jonathan because he's teaching me the same system that George teaches Debby.

Jonathan is as serious about working on the flat as about jumping. He teaches me basic dressage—things like side-stepping, which is making the horse move from side to side. Napoleon, for instance, was very good at controlling his horse—if his horse acted up, he could always straighten it out. At horse shows we have classes where they judge us on the way our ponies walk, trot, and canter on the flat.

You make your horse move forward by squeezing the horse's sides with the calves of your legs. But if you squeeze with only one leg, the horse will move sideways, away from that leg. This is called leg yielding.

Jonathan also teaches a group of us at a nearby indoor riding ring.

About half of the lesson is on the flat and half is jumping.

After I finish riding, whether it's practicing by myself or having a lesson, there's quite a lot of work to be done. I have to cool out Penny and clean her up. I walk her for fifteen minutes without the saddle and with a wool cooler over her. This keeps her from getting a chill.

It's very important that you know these things because it's bad if a horse gets a cold. It's different from getting any old sniffle.

Horses have a very delicate digestive system—it was designed for a grass-eating animal. Also, they moved around a lot on the plains when they were wild. We give them concentrated feed and keep them stabled. Anything upsetting, like getting a chill, or eating or drinking too much when they're hot, can affect their digestive system and give them what is called colic. Colic is like a bad stomach ache. If horses get colic, it's really dangerous because they can die.

Sometimes, when it's hot outside, we give Penny a bath. If I've jumped her, I rub liniment on her legs and bandage them with flannel and cotton. When she's all clean I take her to her stall. If it's chilly I put a sheet on her.

Then I feed her dinner. First I give her hay. Hay is like an appetizer, like a salad before a meal.

Next I mix up her feed. She gets two quarts of sweet feed, two quarts of oats, and vitamins.

And I make sure she has plenty of water. Water is the most important. A horse can drink five to fifteen gallons of water a day.

After everyone's been hayed down and fed, we close the stall doors and say good-night.

We all help out with weekly barn duties. Debby and I usually scrub the buckets while Mark loads fresh bedding for the stalls. Most people think of straw as the usual bedding for horses but we use sawdust instead. It's cheaper and just as good.

Mark and I take turns raking the ring and that's the most fun. We have to do this or else the horses will get rocks in their feet. We all take turns brushing away the cobwebs.

One thing I'm *very* involved with is Pony Club. Sometimes on weekends, or during vacations from school, we go on field trips to breeding farms or other people's stables. These trips are called unmounted meetings. One time we went to Mrs. Debany's farm to see a new foal who was only one week old. He was born three weeks prematurely so he was very tiny. He weighed about seventy-five pounds. They named him Grasshopper. Mrs. Debany told us that the mother of a newborn is very protective, particularly the first week, because she feels she can take care of her foal better than people can. She probably can, too. She'll keep her foal moving as much as possible the first week so it will develop its muscles and get strong. Moving around also helps get the mare's figure back after giving birth. Mares carry for approximately eleven months. They go to a lot of trouble to give birth when no one's looking. The birth only takes about ten minutes.

After the newborn foal is up on its feet, the mother licks it dry. I don't understand how you can lick something dry but cats and horses do it.

A girl is called a filly and a boy is a colt.

A foal can run and keep up with its mother when it's only twenty-four hours old.

On a hot day, when the flies are out, a foal will usually stand next to its mother's tail to take advantage of the swishing. They sure are smart.

It's called a foal until it's weaned, which is in about six months. Then it's called a weanling until it's a year old. Then it's called a yearling. After that they're called two-year-olds, three-year-olds, and so on. Horses can live to be as old as thirty. Ponies usually live a little longer.

Some people think that ponies will grow up to become horses but that isn't so. A pony's foal grows up to be a pony and a horse's foal grows up to be a horse.

Our vet's name is Bill Bradley. He has a special truck, which is refrigerated and has hot and cold running water and an X-ray machine. He comes routinely for things like worming and giving shots, but makes special trips to sign a health certificate for an out-of-state horse show or if one of the horses gets sick.

About twice a year he files down Penny's teeth. This is called floating the teeth. Horses have to have smooth teeth in order to chew their grain. As they chew, their teeth can wear down and form sharp edges which cut their cheeks and tongue. When this happens, they don't chew their food properly and then they have trouble digesting. Penny hates having her teeth floated, and sometimes she puts up a big argument. Dr. Bradley says that he and Penny get along a lot better than they used to.

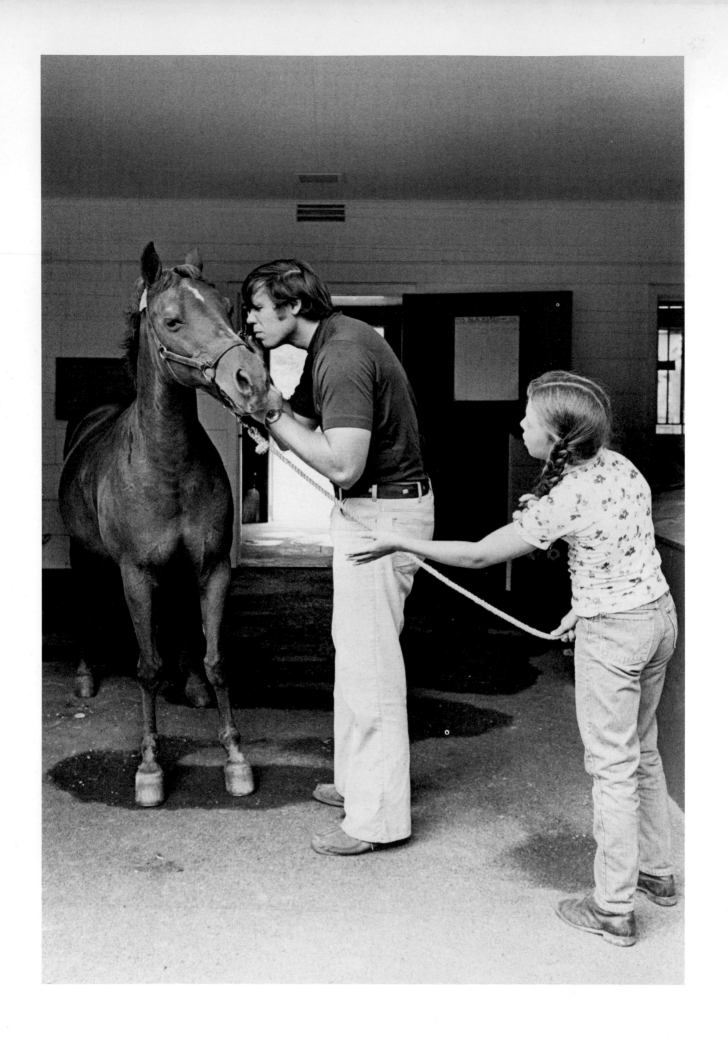

During a regular checkup, he looks at Penny's eyes to be sure her vision is normal.

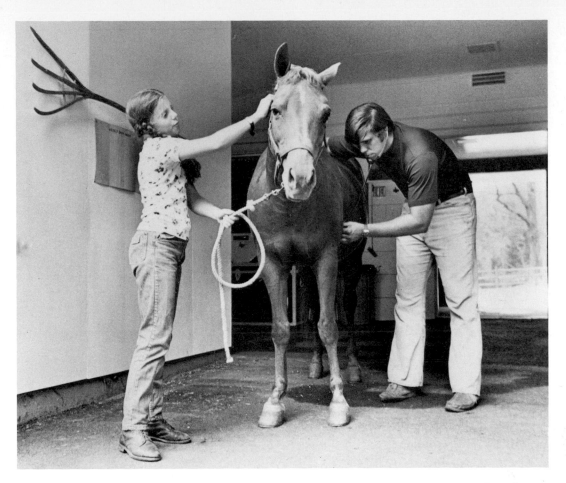

He also listens to her heart and lungs and checks her legs for lameness.

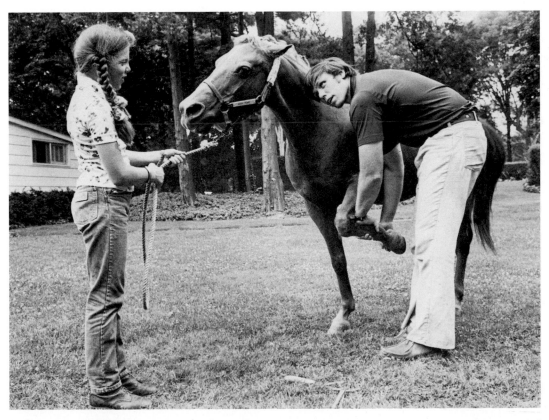

About five years ago Debby thought she wanted to be a vet, so she used to tag along with Dr. Bradley when he went to his different appointments. She really knows what to do when a horse gets cut or a cat gets stepped on. I wouldn't mind being a vet, except for doing operations. I can't stand operations. I think I'd rather be a trainer.

Once a month the farrier comes to shoe all the horses. Or, if a horse throws a shoe, he makes a special trip. His name is Michael Lynch and he's been in the business about thirty years. His father was a farrier and taught him how to do it. It's important to get a farrier who knows what he's doing because a bad one can do real damage to a horse. There are a lot of bad ones because they don't have to take a test or have a license.

The word "farrier" comes from England and means horse-shoe-er. The farrier takes care of the horses' feet only. Lots of people call them blacksmiths by mistake. A blacksmith is the person who does the iron work, which means the steel shaping and the forging. Sometimes Mr. Lynch brings a blacksmith with him but lots of times he does both jobs by himself.

First he takes off the horse's shoes and trims down the hoofs. They grow just like a person's toenails and it's very bad for the horse if they get too big. If their hoofs grow too much, they get clumsy and it can make them lame. It's like wearing a shoe that's too big for you.

After the hoofs are pared down, Mr. Lynch sets up the forge. It has a fan that blows under a fire and gives off very concentrated heat. He puts the shoes in the fire and gets them hot so they get soft and he can bend and shape them. This takes about five minutes after the fire's warmed up and really going.

As each shoe gets red hot, he puts it on an anvil and shapes it with a hammer to fit the horse's foot. When the shoes are cool, Mr. Lynch nails them on. The nails are wedge-shaped so that when you drive them in they come out the side of the hoof. He bends the nails over and files them down. The average shoe gets six nails but there are eight holes if you need that many. A pony like Penny only needs six.

Shoeing doesn't hurt the horse at all if it's done right. Sometimes it hurts the farrier because the horse gets nervous and bites or kicks him. Mr. Lynch has had to go to the hospital lots of times with cracked ribs.

The reason horses need shoes is the same reason people need them — to protect their feet. American Indians used to cover the horses' hoofs with hides from other animals when they took them through mountain areas, over stones. They would tie the hides up around the horses' ankles, just the way they tied their own moccasins.

We go to The Saddler in Wilton, Connecticut, to get stuff repaired and to get riding clothes. Mom also gets presents for our birthdays there. They have all kinds of riding clothes for people: jodhpurs, britches, jackets, hats, boots, shirts, stocks, ties, chokers, and things like garter straps, spurs, and gloves. And for horses they have all kinds of tack: saddles, bridles, and halters, and equipment like sheets, saddle pads, and lead and lunge lines. In fact, they have everything for taking care of a horse, even fly sprays, hoof oil, saddle soap, and ointments for cuts.

When you buy a jacket or jodhpurs, they have you sit on a saddle to see how everything will fit when you're sitting on a horse. When you get boots, they have to measure your feet and your legs too. Mr. Aquino, who owns The Saddler, does the fitting. I get bigger boots than my size to have some growing room.

What I love the most is competing in horse shows around the country. I compete in about fifteen major shows a year—in spring, summer, and fall. I don't show in the winter because most of the good showing is in Florida and I have to be in school.

Showing takes a lot of time, especially getting ready. Before each show I have to clean my tack…clean it really well. First, I clean the leather of my saddle and bridle with saddle soap—this keeps the leather moist so it doesn't crack and break. Then I polish the metal parts of my bridle: the bit, the rings, and all the buckles. Mom says I'm good at that.

Mom makes the shipping bandages for the horses' legs. They protect the horses' legs in shipping when they're in the van and trying to keep their balance. Once Mark and Debby and I got in the back of the van on our hands and knees and Mom drove around so that we'd know what it feels like for the horses. It was very bumpy and we had to keep our balance by shifting our weight. And it was scary not being able to see where we were going.

In the spring, when I'm still in school, most of the horse shows I compete in are on weekends. The first big show of the spring season is Boulder Brook, in the beginning of April. Boulder Brook is near where we live so we don't have to stay in a motel.

The night before a show I try to get to bed early. I set the alarm for around four a.m. I love waking up when it's pitch black outside. You're awake before the whole world and there are no noises — no sounds at all. It's so neat.

Before I go to sleep, I put out the clothes I'll be wearing and I write in my diary.

We van Penny over in the morning. The back of the van has a stall where we can keep her between classes. It's like her home away from home.

I have my own time schedule, which tells me when to have Penny ready for her classes and which ring we're showing in. My brother Mark usually comes along to work as the groom.

The program tells me the class regulations, the judges, and the names of the other competitors. I always look to see which of my friends are showing. It also lists all the different divisions and the ribbons and prizes for each class.

About a half-hour before the class is scheduled to start, I go up to the ring and find Jonathan.

Then I wait with him until it's my turn to compete. He usually reminds me not to get nervous and just to concentrate on the course.

The hunter course consists of a variety of eight jumps. There are usually several post and rails, a gate, a wall, and an in-and-out. We have to jump them in a certain order. They usually display a diagram of the course near the ring. I watch the other horses in the ring and decide how many strides it takes to get from one fence to another. If I'm first in the ring, Jonathan calculates it for me. I hate being first.

Penny and I won quite a few ribbons at Boulder Brook. It's important to be in the ribbons early in the year so that you can qualify for the really big summer shows like Lake Placid and Devon, and the fall shows at Harrisburg and Washington, D.C. You have to have a certain number of points just to enter these shows.

I won some money too. When I win money, I give Mom half to cover my entrance fees and I put the rest into my savings account.

There are six to ten ribbons awarded in each class depending on the show. A blue ribbon, which is the first prize, is assigned five points; a red ribbon, which is second, is three points; yellow, which is third, gets two points; and a white ribbon, which is fourth prize, gets one point. All your points are added up from each class that you win and at the end of the show the horse with the most points in each division is the champion.

Later this spring Penny was the champion at Syracuse, which means she got the highest number of points in her class. They gave us a cooler that said "Pony Champion—Syracuse Horse Show."

During summer, when school's out, we travel to a lot of outdoor shows. They're very fancy and have lots of prestige. Since we're away for a week at a time, we have to pack a tack trunk of stuff like coolers, fly sheets, and grooming equipment.

Last summer we went to Farmington, Devon, Ox Ridge, Fairfield, and Lake Placid. We also went to a few shows on Long Island—Southampton, C. W. Post, and North Shore. Mom or Debby drives the van. When we get to the show grounds, they assign us temporary stalls. They're in big tents and it almost looks like a circus.

As soon as we arrive at the show grounds, I take Penny for a walk to stretch her legs.

When a rider and a pony have been working together for a long time, they kind of develop a language.

After the horses are comfortable and in their stalls, we set up our tack trunk and put up our tack room hangings.

Then we buy a few bales of straw for Penny's bedding and a few bales of hay for her dinner. Penny gets one or two flakes of hay depending on how hard I'm working her. A flake is part of a bale.

I love staying at motels. It's so much fun. Sometimes I can share a room with a friend like Amy Weiss. We play games like "Twenty Questions" and stuff like that. Mom's in a connecting room so we can't be too loud. We get to go out for dinner every night. I like to try different foods that I've never heard of. I also get to watch TV in bed. I like "The Bionic Woman."

On the days we are showing, we try to get to the show grounds around five a.m. because there's a lot to do. First I feed, hay, and water Penny.

Then I get right down to braiding. In olden times horses were braided for the hunt field so their manes and tails wouldn't get tangled in the brambles when they went galloping through the woods. Nowadays it is done for hunter classes to make a horse look fancy and show off its neck and hindquarters.

Sometimes Kym helps. He's a professional braider and can do it a lot faster than I can. He can do about twelve horses a day. Some of the older girls who are showing do braiding to earn extra money.

Braiding tails is not the same as braiding pigtails. It's much harder. Penny's tail is especially hard to do because she has a crooked tail bone.

If it's a rainy day, we do a mud tail. That's when the hairs that normally hang down are doubled up and woven into the braid so they don't get muddy. I *hate* showing in the rain and Penny hates it even more. She actually makes a bad face when she goes out in the rain.

After Penny is braided, I work her on the lunge line for about twenty minutes.

Lungeing exercises her when she's away from home and can't go out and run.

I make her walk, trot, and canter at the end of the line.

Around seven I go and find Jonathan and we school Penny over the jumps she'll have to jump that day. They usually let us practice in the ring. Jonathan goes over the course with me and asks me if I feel all right for the show. We practice the distances between the fences. Then I go back to the tent and wash down Penny. I let her graze for a while.

Next I go up and get my order, which is posted at the gate. They pick the first number for the first class out of a hat. They give you a different order for each class. I like to ride in the middle so I can watch the first people and judge the distances, and then go before the course gets all churned up with hoofprints. They announce the beginning of each class over the loudspeaker—it's called a stable call. There's a thirty-minute call and then a fifteen-minute call.

After I know my order, I like to relax and play checkers with Matthew Burdsall until my first class. When I go into the ring I put a lot of pressure on myself so it's important to take it easy beforehand.

Matthew is my age and rides in most of the shows. He trains with his sister, Katherine. She won the Maclay Finals in Madison Square Garden last year. She's seventeen. Matthew has been riding for a little over a year. Boys usually start riding later than girls. Mom thinks it's because they don't like taking care of horses until they get a little bit older.

As soon as I hear the ringmaster's horn, I know the show is about to start.

Honey Craven was the ringmaster at Devon this year. He's been the ringmaster at Devon and the National Horse Show in Madison Square Garden for umpteen years.

Just before my first class, Mom rebraids my hair. I should be able to do it myself since I can braid Penny's mane, but I'm not very good at it. Mom says I should practice on rainy days. I always wear green and white ribbons because they're my lucky colors.

We get our numbers in the horse show office. You wear the same number throughout the show.

I always wear my Pony Club pin on my riding helmet. You get it when you join.

About ten minutes before I go into the ring, Jonathan goes over the course with me one more time. Then I warm up in the schooling area next to the ring for about five minutes. This time is very important because I find out what kind of mood my pony's in and I get used to jumping. It's like in baseball when the pitcher goes into the warm-up cage or when the batter swings a few bats. I have to get really used to finding the distance or place for my pony to leave the ground.

I love the schooling area at Lake Placid the best because the trees are so beautiful.

When the paddock master calls my number the first time, I know I only have a few minutes before my round. They call you three times in all. The first gets you up near the ring. The second is for you to get on deck. And the third is to enter the ring. They have a one-minute rule. If you're not in the ring within one minute after they call your number the third time, you're eliminated. That's never happened to me.

Jonathan gives me last-minute instructions except when I'm nervous and then he leaves me alone.

While I'm on deck, Mom touches up Penny's hoofs with hoof oil.

Then I wait in the starting gate for my number to be called the final time.

Jonathan always watches me and sometimes George Morris does too.

The person who's watching me the closest is the judge. Charles Dennehy is from Lake Forest, Illinois, and he judges many of the top shows throughout the country.

I love the schooling and all the practice, but what I love most is the moment in the ring when you have to give it your all.

After I finish in the ring, I dismount and Jonathan comes right over to tell me what I could have done better. Once in a while he says it was perfect, but not very often.

After everyone has ridden in the class, they call back the ten ponies who've had the best rounds to the center of the ring. They do this to make sure the ponies are sound in case someone has jumped a lame pony. Lameness doesn't really show when they're jumping but when they're jogged out for soundness it will.

Then they award the ribbons.

If you win, one of the show photographers usually takes your picture. George Axt has been taking pictures at horse shows for twenty years. He lives in a camper and travels to all the shows. He also takes video tapes of people riding. He develops and prints right in his trailer. He has a funny hat that he throws into the air to make the horses put their ears forward.

Although most of my classes are pony hunter, where Penny's being judged, I usually ride in one or two equitation classes on the flat. In those classes they are judging *my* form. We all go into the ring at the same time and the judge makes us walk, trot, and canter. Then there are certain individual tests that the judge can ask of his top choices before he makes his final decision. The ringmaster always says, "Don't bunch together—spread out!" But we always *do* bunch up.

Debby did very well this year. She rides in the junior jumper classes. These are classes that are judged on how high and how fast her horse can jump and maneuver a small tight course. My pony hunter classes are judged on how evenly I can jump my eight fences. Debby's fences can go up to five feet but mine can't be higher than two and a half feet.

I love it if I happen to be nearby when George talks to Debby about riding.

Debby and I usually try and watch each other's rounds if we don't have classes at the same time, and then we can talk about how we thought they went. Sometimes if I feel discouraged, Debby tells me that she made the same mistakes when she was my age.

One of the most exciting parts of the horse show circuit is getting to see the famous riders like Rodney Jenkins. I can learn a lot just watching him school his horses.

I really like Rodney. He's been riding since he was seven and now he's a professional. Sometimes he rides his own horse but mostly he rides other people's for them.

I got his autograph this year at Devon.

They always have a lead-line class at Devon. It's for little kids who are usually going into the show ring for the first time and it's very funny. I was in the lead-line classes five years ago on my first pony, called Fifi. She was a chestnut Shetland pony and she was only eight hands high.

At the end of the class everyone got lollypops.

When I'm not in classes or watching the show, I like to go around with my friend Meg Brown. Her older brother, Buddy, is on the United States Olympic Team. Meg usually rides her pony but this summer she couldn't because her pony had just foaled. Her family has a trailer, which they live in when they're on the road showing.

I love cotton candy but it's so fattening. When I get older like Debby, I'll have to go on a diet. Debby's always on a diet or else George gets after her. Once she went on a pure liquid diet and almost fainted in school. I have to watch my weight now a little bit. You don't want to get too heavy for your pony. There's nothing uglier than a fat rider on a horse. It's important to eat a lot of vitamins and protein to keep your energy up.

There's a man named Seaweed who goes to all the horse shows, starting with Florida in the winter. His specialty is bacon and egg sandwiches. He sells a lot of cheeseburgers too. At Ox Ridge he sold 10,000. He used to be a good rider. He also works on the jump crew putting up jumps. And sometimes he even runs the gate.

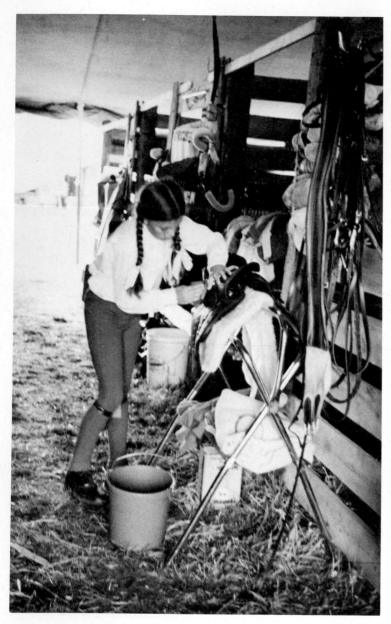

Each day at a show is a little different, but I always finish up by cleaning my tack and mucking out the stall.

Then I feed Penny, and Mom and I head back to the motel for a good night's sleep before another day of showing.

By the middle of August most of the summer shows are over. Both Debby and I did well this summer. Debby qualified for the Maclay Finals and we both qualified for Harrisburg and Washington, D.C.

They send you a notice of acceptance in the mail.

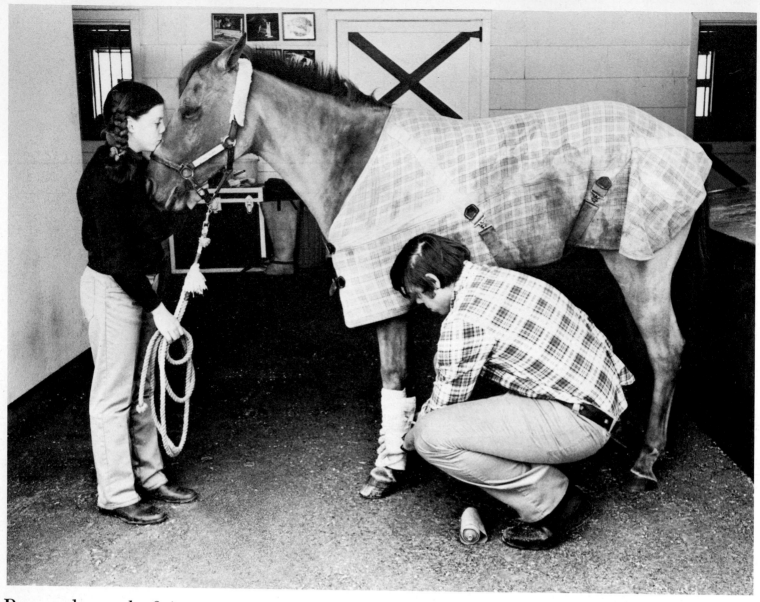

But at the end of August, a most terrible thing happened! One day while we were schooling, Penny went lame. Dr. Bradley came over and said that she had hurt her tendon. He bandaged her leg with a gel cast and gave her a shot. He said that her leg needed complete rest and that I couldn't ride her for at least a few months. I felt awful.

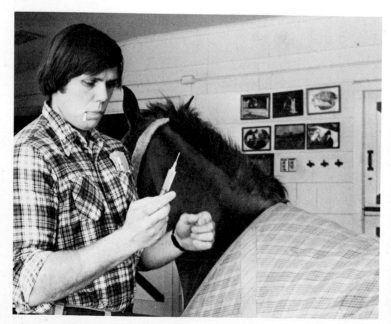

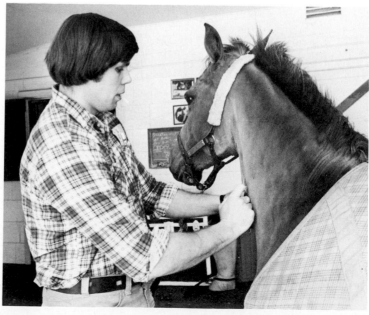

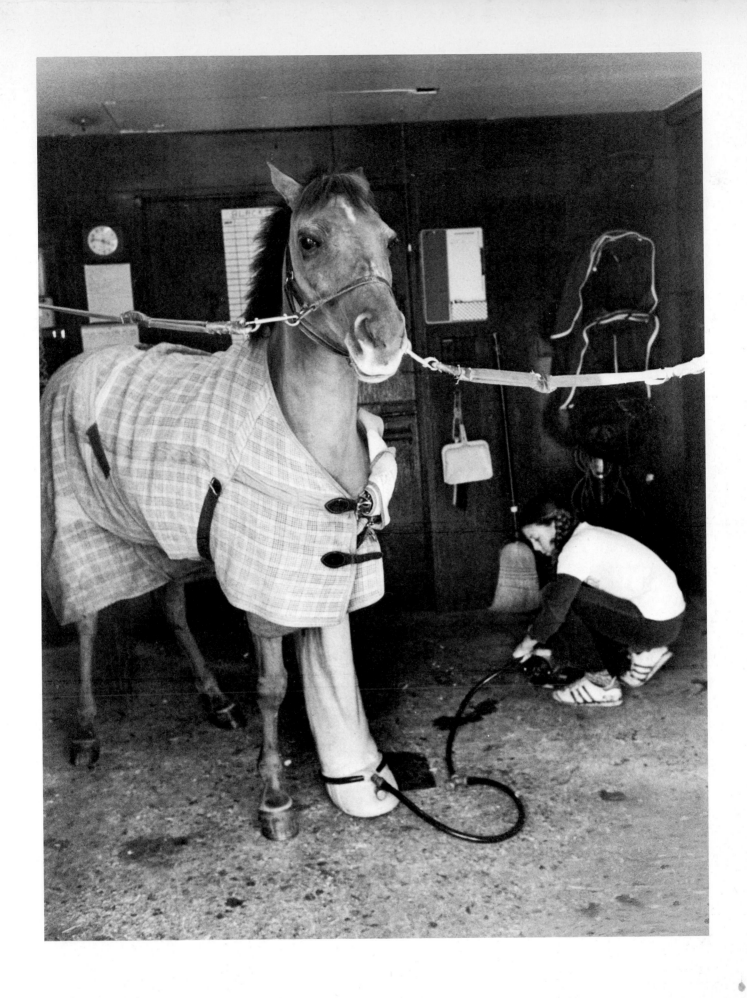

Dr. Bradley took off the cast in a few days and I gave her a whirlpool treatment every day for several weeks. She made wonderful progress and finally was good as new. Thank goodness! But I still couldn't take her to Harrisburg or Washington.

Once a year, in August, there's a Pony Club rally and I'd also been looking forward to riding Penny in that. Since she was lame, I borrowed another pony from friends.

Each region has its own rally. Debby, Mark, and I are members of the Greenwich Pony Club, which is part of the Metropolitan Region. It's the only time in riding that I compete as part of a team instead of as an individual. We ride in a team, the same way they do at the Olympics. Each team competes in a number of events: dressage, cross country, and stadium jumping. The team that gets the most points wins. Unlike riders in the Olympics, we have to take a written test and we're also judged on stable management.

Mark was our captain and the other members of our team were Joan Levee and Jimmy Kingery. Mark kept complaining that it was hard to be captain of us kids because we never listened to him.

The rally only lasts one day and starts around eight in the morning. Mom was the rally coordinator and Jack Graham was the overall judge. The rally begins with a call to order. We're told that before any of the events, we'll have an inspection of our vans and tack. No one is allowed to help us or even talk to us, or we get points taken off.

My favorite event is cross country because you go out by yourself and have to ride over rough terrain. You have to get to the finish line within a certain number of minutes or you're eliminated. The time allowed is usually very fast so the ride is always exciting. Debby was one of the official judges making a safety check at the starting line. This is the final check over all the tack to make sure it's adjusted properly, is clean and in good condition.

When I was ready to go, the timekeeper recorded my starting time. I had a clear run and I finished in nine minutes. They have judges posted at all the jumps in the woods. If your horse refuses a jump, they mark down a fault on their score cards.

After the summer is over, it's back to school. The horses get a good rest and we all take a breather before Debby gets ready for Madison Square Garden in November.

We usually clean and repaint all the tack trunks.

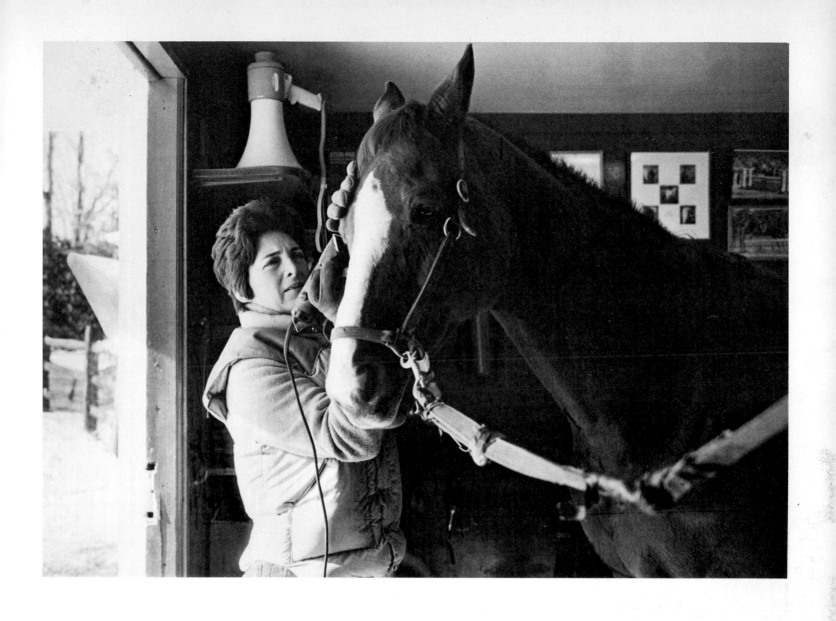

We also have to clip Debby's horse because you can't show a horse with a shaggy coat in the Garden.

The National in the Garden is the most exciting horse show of all! This year I went to the opening night with Jonathan. He was all dressed up. The show lasts for a week and there are classes all day and then more at night. Mom usually lets me take a day or two off from school because it only happens once a year.

Lots of famous horse people come to watch. I saw Kathy Kusner, who is one of my idols. She made the United States Equestrian Team when she was twenty-one and rode in the Olympics three times. Then she became a steeplechase jockey. She got her first pony when she was twelve years old and used to sell pony rides on him so he could be self-supporting. I also saw Bert de Nemethy, who is the coach of the U.S.E.T. Gordon Wright was there too. He trained George Morris, William Steinkraus, and lots of other famous riders. He still teaches but not as much as he used to.

Victor Hugo-Vidal, a very famous rider and trainer, is always the main announcer.

There was a big marching band, which was very loud. The whole Garden was draped with bunting and flags from all the nations competing in the international classes.

Then there was a parade of teams. The United States Equestrian Team has four members—Frank Chapot, who is captain, Michael Matz, Buddy Brown, and Dennis Murphy. When each team rode out, the band played its national anthem. This year there were seven international teams and they came from Australia, Belgium, Canada, Holland, Ireland, Puerto Rico, and the United States. A team can have one to four members.

It would be so exciting to ride with the U.S.E.T. There aren't any women on the team now but there have been quite a few in the past. I hope I can make it when I grow up.

One of my favorite events was an exhibition by the Royal Canadian Mounted Police. I love to watch them perform. They do all kinds of maneuvers, with names like "Clover Leaf" and "Threading the Needle," in time to music. While we were watching, Jonathan explained to me that even though the drills looked very complicated, they were all made up of separate dressage movements he and I had worked on together.

The horses are all matched bays and each one has a maple leaf stenciled on its hindquarters. This is done by laying the stencil of the leaf on its rump and brushing the hair the wrong way with a wet brush.

And all of the horses' manes are clipped except for one. That's the horse that Queen Elizabeth rides when she visits Canada.

The Mounties wear ceremonial scarlet tunics and carry lances.

I counted thirty-two of them.

Buddy Brown rode throughout the week and I got to watch him a lot. He's the youngest rider on the team.

This year the United States won the Nations Cup for the fifth time, which means they get to keep the trophy. Buddy won quite a few ribbons.

Afterwards I went back to the stabling area to see him.

On Saturday afternoon Debby was one of eleven riders called into the middle of the ring. They were the high-point winners of the year in the Professional Horseman's Association Equitation Trophy. Victor Hugo-Vidal gave her a ribbon, a silver dish, and a kiss! The whole family came to the Garden, including my grandparents.

On the last day of the show, Debby rode in the Maclay Finals. There were 159 competitors from twenty-six states in her class. She didn't win anything but George told her she rode well and that's the most important thing. The girl who did win is another one of George's students. Her name is Colette Lozins and she's only sixteen years old. George won both the Maclay and the Medal when he was only fourteen. Nobody else has ever done that. Debby still has one more year to try for the title.

I hope I get to ride in the Garden some day.

After the Garden, Jonathan told me that I really should think about selling Penny because I was getting too big for her. I knew it was for my own good, but it made me very sad to think of saying goodbye to a pony I love.

Mom, Debby, and I went to see some bigger ponies. Mara Tarnapol, one of our neighbors, had a nice one. It was the perfect size for me, and I liked riding her a lot.

Another thing that happened was that Fifi, who was my very first pony, came home for a visit. Our neighbors have a little girl who is learning to ride on Fifi. I'm glad that the people who have her now live next door so I can see her sometimes.

Another family nearby—the Pedersens—wanted Penny for their little girl named Muffy. Muffy is smaller than I am and is just starting to show in pony classes. I took her for a ride on the lead line so she could try Penny out.

Afterwards we had a talk, and I told Muffy what Penny's feed is and the things she likes and doesn't like—such as how she loves to be scratched behind her ears.

Penny will be perfect for her. They will give Penny lots of love and the best of care.

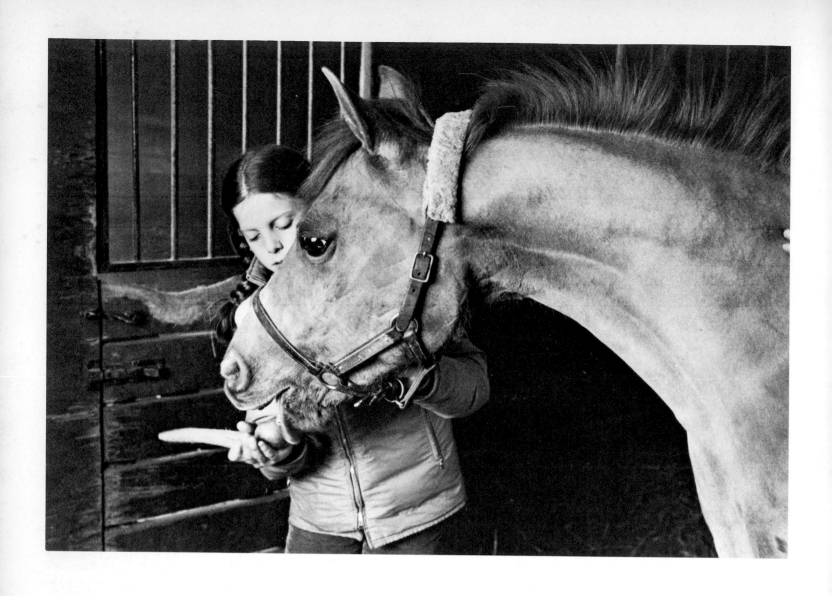

On the night before Penny left for her new home, I went down to the barn. I gave her some apples and carrots. I told her how much I loved her and that we would see each other in the spring at all the shows. And then I kissed her goodbye.

That night when I went to bed, I cried. Mom said that I shouldn't feel too sad because Penny was going to such a nice family and because Christmas was coming soon.

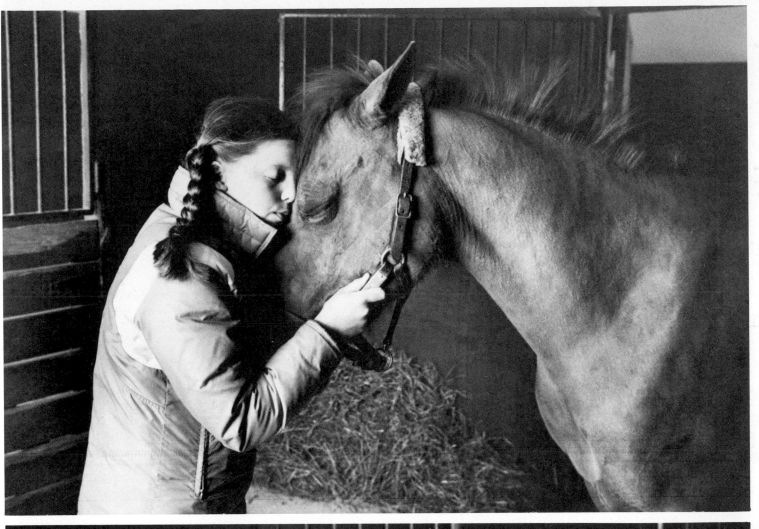
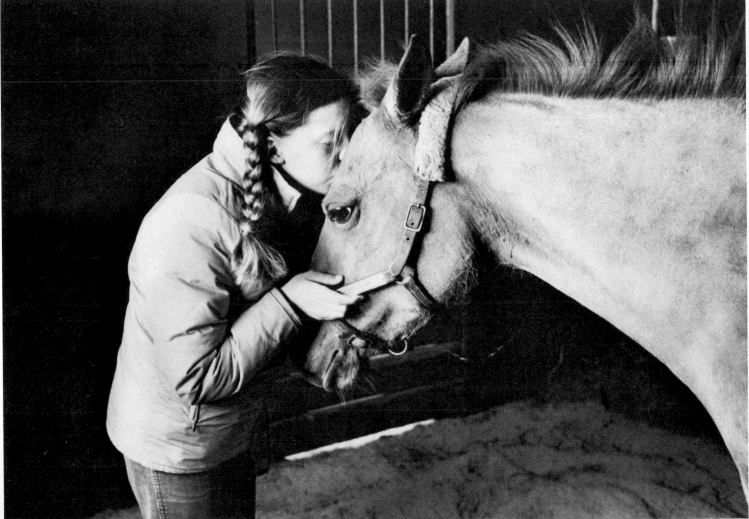

On Christmas morning Mom came into my room very early with two presents. Normally we all wait until after breakfast but Mom was so excited she couldn't wait.

I opened the first box and couldn't believe it. Inside was a brand new show halter and a note from Mom and Dad.

The note said: *"We couldn't fit your new pony into this box but she's waiting for you in the barn."*

Then she gave me a present from my grandparents…a beautiful green and white horse blanket with my initials on it.

I must have gotten dressed in two seconds. I ran down to the barn with the halter and blanket as fast as I could.

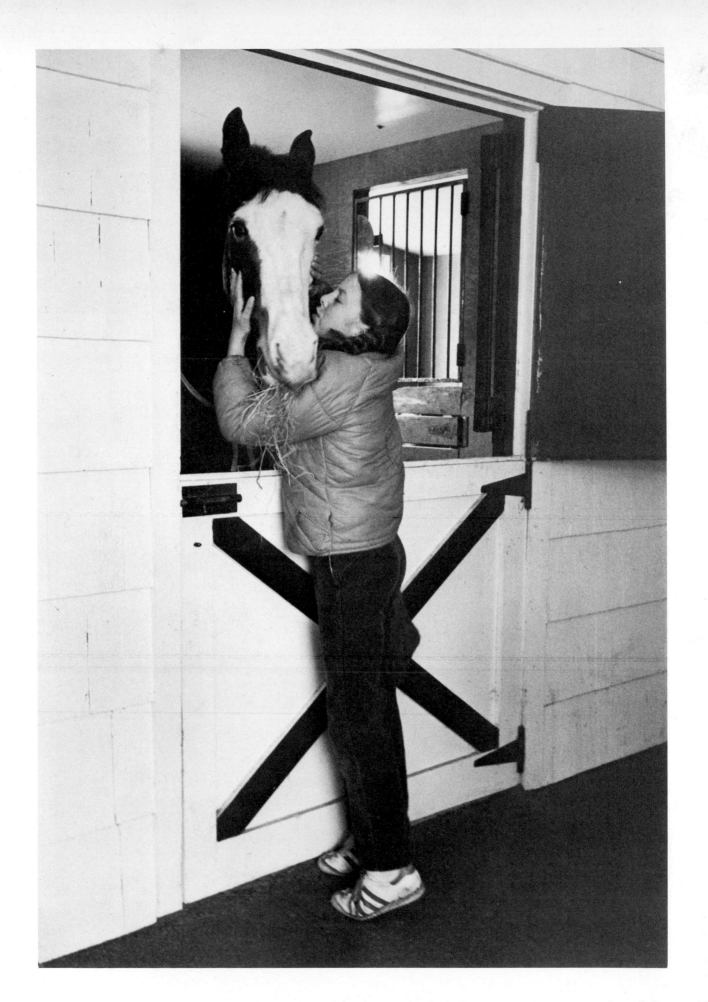

There was a new pony waiting for me in the stall. Of course I recognized her right away. She had a red ribbon tied around her neck. I ran up and gave her a big hug and a kiss. I could tell that we were going to get along together just fine.

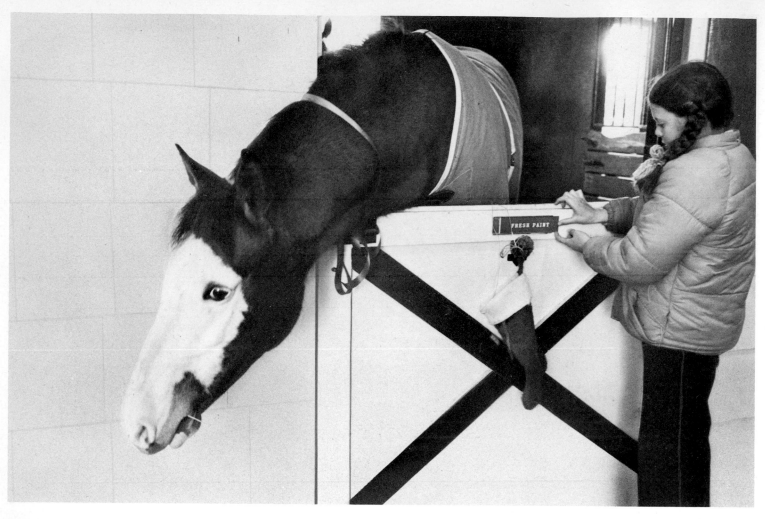

There was a new name plate in the slot on the door. It said "Fresh Paint." It's a perfect name for her because she looks as if she has a splash of white paint on her face.

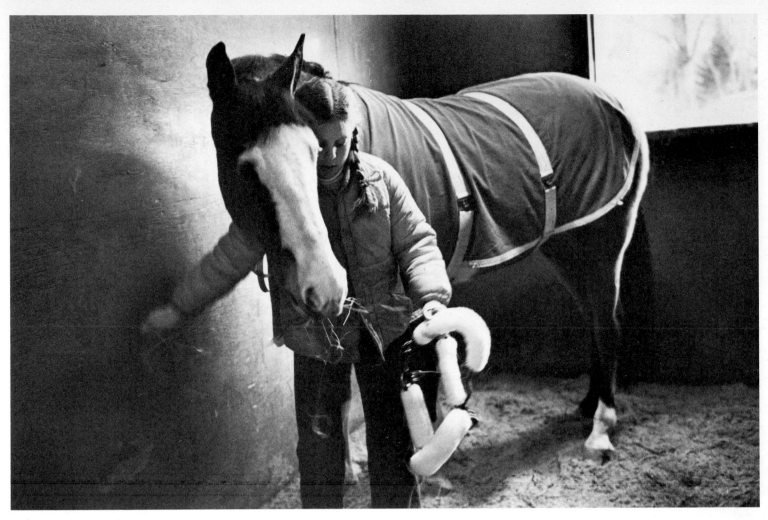

I put the new halter and blanket on her. Then I walked her outside and admired her. She's 14 hands, which means I'll show her in the large pony division.

Mom and Dad came out to see us. I hugged them both and they helped me up on her.

Afterwards I took Paint, which is what I'll call her, for a little run in the snow. I told her what an exciting year we had ahead of us.

I hope we'll have as many good times together as Penny and I did.

# *Acknowledgments*

The question that everyone asks me is "How did you find Vivi?" I began this book by doing a lot of research. The first step was a visit to M. J. Knoud Saddlery Shop on Madison Avenue, where I bought a pile of books and magazines. I felt it was important that before I started looking for a child, I should have some idea of the qualifications he or she should meet. Next, I had lunch with James Fallon, executive director of the American Horse Shows Association, and he, in turn, arranged an introduction to George Morris. I drove out to Hunterdon Stables in New Jersey and watched George teach. He had one student, Martha Wachtel, who was particularly helpful, telling me about the various horse shows. She told me to come to Boulder Brook the following weekend.

I found Vivi Malloy at the Boulder Brook Horse Show. It was cold and windy and I stood watching as child after child entered the ring. Vivi had just been pinned and she had a quality that appealed to me. I followed her and "Penny" down to their van and took some pictures. Vivi seemed to accept my presence without question; in fact, within minutes I was holding her pony for her. I hung around for the remainder of the day—observing, taking pictures, and meeting the rest of the family—and came back the next day. That evening I called her mother and explained what I would like to do, and Mrs. Malloy said she would discuss it with Vivi and the others in the family. Vivi actually had some reservations. She thought it might interfere with her concentration, but when she thought about it some more, she decided that she could probably handle it, providing I promised not to talk to her while she was getting ready to show. I agreed.

I spent roughly a year following Vivi with my camera and notebook to horse shows around the country. I was with her when she won and when she lost. The two worst things about working on this book were having to get up at four a.m. when she was showing, and being beaten at checkers every time we played.

There are so many people to thank. When I began this book I knew so little about horses and without the expertise of those who knew and were willing to share their knowledge with me, I would have been lost. I am particularly grateful to Jonathan Devine, William Steinkraus, Nancy Nicholas, Anne Freedgood, and Debby Malloy, who helped me with the editing. They spent hours and hours with me as I worked over my notes and pictures. I am also grateful to my editor, Robert Gottlieb. He was perhaps the only person involved who knew less about horses than I did, so he made me feel that if I could make him understand what the book was all about, then maybe I was getting somewhere after all.

I would also like to thank all the people who read the manuscript and looked at the layout in various stages and offered valuable suggestions. They are Chuck and Maggie Elliott, Nancy and Bonnie Wright, Joan Stanton, Judy Minetree, Torrance York, Margo Lord, Cheryl Rossum, M.A. Stoneridge, Regina Scudellari, Michael Friedman, Julia Freedgood, and Vicky Wilson. My assistant, June Makela, helped me from beginning to end. So did Kurt Vonnegut. Jim Lipton lent me dozens of books for research, gave good advice, and was also brave enough to give me my first riding lesson at the Topping Stables. Geraldine Shephard and Deke August helped me with my accreditation at Madison Square Garden. It seems that almost everyone on the twenty-first floor of Knopf was involved in some way with this book—Martha Kaplan, Jane Friedman, Bill Loverd, Kathy Hourigan, Anne McCormick, Debbie Phillips, Maria Temechko, Barbara Rulison, Bill Koshland, Nina Bourne—the list goes on and on but everyone was always wonderful to me.

For me, the best part of doing these books—the part I really enjoy—is when I get into the production end. That's when all the pictures have been taken, edited, and worked into their sequence; the writing is finished, and we move into the mechanical process of sizing the pictures and making words fit. Bob Scudellari and Elissa Ichiyasu designed this book, as they did *A Very Young Dancer.* Working with them, from beginning to end, is always a total joy. I am indebted to Neal Jones and Becky Mlynarczyk for their skilled copy-editing; and to Marylea O'Reilly, Ellen McNeilly, and Marta Gutman for their production genius.

Last of all, I would like especially to thank the entire Malloy family and all the other people whose pictures appear in these pages for letting me share this past year with them. Without them, this book would not be.

—Jill Krementz

# Down the Colorado

*Long ago, there was a great wise chief, who mourned the death of his wife, and would not be comforted until Ta-vwoats, one of the Indian gods, came to him, and told him she was in a happier land, and offered to take him there, that he might see for himself, if, upon his return, he would cease to mourn. The great chief promised. Then Ta-vwoats made a trail through the mountains that intervene between that beautiful land, the balmy region in the great west, and this, the desert home of the poor Nú-ma.*

*This trail was the canyon gorge of the Colorado. Through it he led him; and, when they had returned, the deity exacted from the chief a promise that he would tell no one of the joys of that land, lest, through discontent with the circumstances of this world, they should desire to go to heaven. Then he rolled a river into the gorge, a mad, raging stream, that should engulf any that might attempt to enter thereby.*

*More than once have I been warned by the Indians not to enter this canyon. They considered it disobedience to the gods and contempt for their authority, and believed that it would surely bring upon me their wrath.*

*—John Wesley Powell*
*1869*

# Down the Colorado

John Wesley Powell
Diary of the First Trip
Through the Grand Canyon
1869

Eliot Porter
Photographs and Epilogue
1969

Foreword and Notes by Don D. Fowler

 E. P. Dutton & Co., Inc. | New York | 1969

Published, 1969, in the United States by E. P. Dutton & Co., Inc., New York, and simultaneously in Canada by Clarke, Irwin & Co., Ltd., Toronto and Vancouver

First Edition

Library of Congress Catalog Card Number: 70-77353

Portions of John Wesley Powell's diary were first published in *Scribner's Monthly* in 1874-75 and in book form under the title, *Explorations of the Colorado River of the West and Its Tributaries* (1875).

Grateful acknowledgment is made for permission to quote from the following sources:
*The Anthropology of the Numa: John Wesley Powell's Manuscripts on Great Basin Indians,* Don D. Fowler and Catherine S. Fowler (eds.), Smithsonian Contributions to Anthropology, *in press, 1969.*
*A Canyon Voyage,* by Frederick S. Dellenbaugh, issued as a Yale Western Americana Paperbound, July, 1962, by Yale University Press, New Haven, Connecticut.

The etchings and drawings reproduced herewith are from the collections of the National Park Service, United States National Museum, and the National Collection of Fine Arts.

Beaman photographs appear on pages 27, 33, 40, 42, 44, 45, 49, 67, 121.
Hiller photographs appear on pages 57, 75, 77, 96, 102, 130.
Geological Survey photographs appear on pages 60, 110, 111, 130.

Photographs not otherwise credited are the work of Eliot Porter.

Produced in association with Chanticleer Press, Inc., New York,
and printed at Amilcare Pizzi—S.P.A. Milan, Italy.

A08830

# Contents

Foreword by Don D. Fowler                                        9

John Wesley Powell:
Diary of the First Trip Through the Grand Canyon               25
1869

From Green River City to Flaming Gorge                         27

From Flaming Gorge to the Gate of Lodore                       36

The Canyon of Lodore                                          42

From Echo Park to the Mouth of the Uinta River                52

From the Mouth of the Uinta River
to the Junction of the Grand and Green                        63

From the Junction of the Grand and Green
to the Mouth of the Little Colorado                           77

The Grand Canyon of the Colorado                             107

Eliot Porter:
The Canyons of the Colorado — Past and Present               147
1969

Index                                                        167

# Foreword

I

On May 24, 1869, a small group of onlookers at Green River Station, Wyoming Territory, waved and cheered good-by as ten men in four specially built boats rowed out onto the Green River to begin an epic journey southward into the relatively unknown Canyon Country of the Colorado River. Their aim was to run the Green to its confluence with the Grand River, where the two streams meet to form the Colorado, then down the Colorado to the foot of Grand Canyon.

The leader of the party was a small, bearded man who had lost his right arm at Shiloh, but whose courage and determination more than compensated for the inconvenience of having only one hand. This man was John Wesley Powell.

On August 30, 1869, some thirteen weeks after the start of the trip, Powell and six men in two boats emerged from the Grand Canyon at the confluence of the Virgin and Colorado rivers to find some men fishing with nets for their remains. Powell and his men had been several times reported drowned, and the men were under orders from Brigham Young, the Mormon leader, to look for any trace of them. One man had left the party near the beginning of the trip and three others had left at Separation Rapids in the depths of the Grand Canyon. These men, O. G. and Seneca Howland and William Dunn, refused to continue on and had climbed out onto the north rim of the canyon —to be killed three days later by Shivwits Paiute Indians. One boat was lost in the rapids of the Green and a second was abandoned after the three men left.

Powell returned to the East a hero and had the enjoyment of reading his own obituaries along the way. He went to Washington and obtained a Congressional appropriation to make a second trip down the river. The appropriation in effect established the fourth of the "Great Surveys," the Geographical and Geological Survey of the Rocky Mountain Region, J. W. Powell in Charge, which, under federal sponsorship, were mapping and exploring the West. The other surveys under Clarence King, F. V. Hayden, and Lt. George Wheeler were already under way. Ultimately, in 1879, the King, Hayden, and Powell surveys would be merged into the United States Geological Survey. Powell would become Director of the Survey in 1881.

The second river trip was made in the summer of 1871 from Green River Station to Lonely Dell (soon to be renamed Lee's Ferry), and in 1872 from that point to the mouth of Kanab Creek in Grand Canyon. No attempt was made to continue on to the mouth of the Virgin River as before. During this second trip photographs were made on large-format wet-plate negatives, first by E. O. Beaman and in 1872 by James Fennemore and John K. (Jack) Hillers. Some of these are included herein.

The two river trips mark the beginning of Powell's association with the Canyon Country of the Colorado River. Throughout the 1870's Powell and his men mapped the area and studied its geology and its Indian inhabitants. Powell's first contact with the Indians of the Canyon Country was in the winter of 1868–69. While he was scouting the Green River country in preparation for his first river trip, he camped near a band of "Tabuats" Utes on the White River in northwestern Colorado. Here he began to learn the Ute-Southern Paiute language, observed curing ceremonies and other rituals, and began to collect the myths and tales told by the old people to while away the long winter evenings. The Indians named him "Kapurats," meaning "Arm Off," a name he is still referred to by some of the Southern Paiute people of northern Arizona. He continued his studies of the Indians of the region throughout the 1870's. During that time his interest expanded to include all North American Indians. This interest culminated in 1879 in the formation of the Bureau of Ethnology (after 1894, the Bureau of American Ethnology), which Powell directed from its inception until his death in 1902.

The geological studies made by Powell and his men—Powell on the Colorado canyon and the Uinta Mountains, Clarence Dutton on the Grand Canyon, and G. K. Gilbert on the Henry Mountains— remain classics in the field. As we noted, Powell was to become Director of the United States Geological Survey in 1881, a post he held concurrently with the Directorship of the Bureau of Ethnology until 1894.

When Powell embarked on the first river trip in 1869 he had determined to continue a budding, though short, career as a professional geologist and natural historian. As a young man he had developed a strong interest in natural history, especially in shells and fossils. He had gone on expeditions, usually alone, including long skiff-trips down the Ohio, the Illinois, and the upper Mississippi rivers and hiking trips across parts of Wisconsin, Illinois, and Ohio, collecting specimens

River rapids are the opposite of sea waves and remain in one place while the water flows through. In many rapids there is an eddy on each side of this tail in which a current runs up-river with great force. Thus, if a boat is caught in an eddy, it may be carried a second time through part of the rapid.

as he went. On one walking trip across lower Michigan he visited relatives in Detroit. There he met his first cousin and future wife, Emma Dean.

Powell's schooling was sporadic and of short duration. He taught school off and on and worked as a farmer in between. At the beginning of the Civil War he enlisted in the 20th Illinois Volunteers as a private. He soon rose to the rank of Captain, and later Major, an honorary rank he retained throughout his life. He became an artillery officer and something of an expert on fortifications. Soon after the 20th Illinois were mustered into federal service, Powell obtained a brief leave, went to Detroit, married Emma Dean, and returned with her to the fighting. At Shiloh his right arm was shattered by a Confederate minnie ball and was subsequently amputated just below the elbow. Emma nursed him back to health and he returned to the war, participating in the siege of Vicksburg and several other engagements.

After the war Powell returned to Bloomington, Illinois, to become Professor of Geology at Illinois Wesleyan University, but soon moved across town to Illinois State Normal University. He also was active in the Illinois State Natural History Society, another organization that helped to support his early explorations.

In 1867 Powell led a natural history expedition to the Rocky Mountains west of Denver. The party, composed of volunteer students, friends, and colleagues, had intended to go to the Black Hills but was diverted southward by rumors of Indian troubles. In 1868 Powell again led a party of volunteers to the Rockies. Powell and some members of the party climbed Long's Peak, the first recorded ascent. In the early fall, the party journeyed westward to the White River where Powell, Emma, and three others were to spend the winter. The rest of the party turned north to the railroad in Wyoming and returned to Illinois.

Powell spent the winter exploring the Green River country. Based on what he saw, together with what he was able to learn from the reports of others, he decided that the Canyon Country could be explored by boat. In late January of 1869 he wrote to the President of Illinois Normal University:

I have explored the canyon of the Green where it cuts through the foot of the Uintah Mountains, and find that boats can be taken down. So that the prospects for making the passage of the "Grand Canyon" of the Colorado is still brighter. The canyon of the Green was said to be impassable. (Quoted in E. S. Watson [ed.], *The Professor Goes West*...[Bloomington, Ill., 1954], p. 24.)

Red lobelia at Wilson Canyon.

In the early spring Powell returned to the East and gained some support for his venture, though not the federal aid he had hoped for. He had four boats built to his specifications and shipped to Green River Station on the newly completed transcontinental railroad. He collected a party of volunteers and embarked on his first river trip.

## II

When Powell began his trip, contemporary maps had a large blank space from the upper Green to the confluence of the Colorado and Virgin rivers. Although the maps indicated *terra incognita,* the country had been explored by White men as early as A.D. 1540, and occupied by Indians as early as A.D. 400, if not before. What remained unknown in May of 1869 were the exact courses of the Green and Colorado rivers and their navigability. Powell had heard stories of whirlpools and rapids that would swallow or destroy boats in an instant. He had heard other stories of the river sinking underground to emerge hundreds of miles away. Some men claimed to have navigated parts of the river system. In 1867 one James White had floated out of the Grand Canyon on a jerry-built raft. To the Mormon settlers at Callville who found him he told a story of having escaped from some Indians up the river and floating through the Grand Canyon on his raft. The settlers nursed him and thought him mad.

There were other, similar stories, but few facts. The only verified river trip of any extent had been made in 1825 by General (of the Missouri militia) William Ashley, one of the owners of the American Fur Company, and some of his men. They floated in bullboats and dugout canoes down the Green from Sandy Creek in Wyoming to the mouth of the Duchesne River in the Uinta Basin. Beyond that point the exact course of the Green was unknown for many years, although Ashley was able to establish that it was not an affluent of the Columbia as some had thought.

The mystery of the Colorado River and the Canyon Country had fascinated, and sometimes repelled, men long before Ashley or Powell. By A.D. 400, and perhaps earlier, Anasazi Pueblo peoples, probably among the ancestors of the present-day Hopi, were farming along the river terraces and in the tributary canyons of the San Juan River, in Glen and Grand canyons of the Colorado, and along the Virgin River. The Grand Canyon was also occupied by carriers of the Cohonina culture, some of whom may have been the ancestors of the Havasupai Indians who still live in the area.

Farther north, above Cataract Canyon along the Grand and Green rivers and their tributaries, the Fremont peoples lived, from about A.D. 700 to 1200. These people, the probable ancestors of the present-day Navajo and Apache peoples, were also farmers, having learned the art from the Anasazi to the south. Both peoples hunted mountain sheep and deer and collected wild seeds and roots in the canyons. Then around A.D. 1200–1300, for reasons not fully understood by archeologists, the Fremont and the Anasazi peoples withdrew from the Canyon Country. The Fremont peoples apparently moved eastward onto the High Plains, then turned southward into what is now Texas, Mexico, and New Mexico. The Anasazi withdrew southward and eastward toward the Hopi mesas, some continuing onward to the headwaters of the Rio Grande. As Powell and his men passed through the Canyon Country, they found petroglyphs and house-ruins, traces of the former occupants whom Powell called "Shinumo," a term for the Hopi.

The Fremont and Anasazi peoples were replaced by the Ute-Southern Paiute Indians who moved into the region from the Great Basin to the west, probably between A.D. 1000 and 1500.

The first White men to explore the Canyon Country were part of the Spanish expedition of 1540–42 led by Francisco Vásquez de Coronado. The first contact with the lower Colorado, well below the Grand Canyon, was made by Hernando de Alarcón. To supply the Coronado party, Alarcón's ships sailed up the Sea of Cortes (Gulf of California) on the mistaken assumption that Coronado's journey would be parallel to, and near, the Sea of Cortes. Unable to get his ships across the estuary at the mouth of the Colorado, Alarcón explored the river by rowboat, as far as the confluence of the Gila, looking in vain for Coronado. Meanwhile, Coronado and his men had reached the Zuni settlement of Hawikuh in what is now western New Mexico. There they learned of Tusayan, the Zuni name for the Hopi villages to the west. Captain Pedro de Továr was sent to investigate. The Hopi told Továr about a great river to the west. Továr returned to Hawikuh and reported this news to Coronado, who sent Captain López de Cárdenas and a small party of men to investigate. The river was important because it might lead them to Alarcón. Cárdenas and his men finally reached the south rim of the Grand Canyon, thus becoming the first White men to see that sublime spectacle. They tried to climb down to the river but could not. Though possibly impressed by the magnificence of the region,

Cárdenas and his men returned to Hawikuh and reported to Coronado that it was a "useless piece of country."

The Spaniards ignored the Grand Canyon and whatever lay beyond it for the next one hundred and twenty-five years. During that time their activities were principally confined to present-day New Mexico and southern Arizona. Only the lower Colorado River, from the estuary to the foot of Black Canyon, was explored; among the Spanish explorers was Fray Eusebio Francisco Kino, a Jesuit missionary, who made his explorations from 1694 to 1710.

One reason for the lack of Spanish exploration into the upper Colorado River area was a drawn-out period of warfare with the Southern Ute who dominated the mountains to the north and west of Santa Fé. But peace was made in 1750, and soon after Spanish trappers and traders from Santa Fé and Abiquiu began exploring the San Juan, Dolores, Uncompahgre, and Gunnison tributaries of the Colorado. Though many trips were made, few were documented, one such being that of Don Juan María de Rivera from Santa Fé to the Gunnison River in 1765.

In 1776 a Franciscan priest, Francisco Hermenegildo Garcés, was led by a Havasupai trader from the lower Colorado to Havasupai Canyon and the Grand Canyon, thus becoming the first Spaniard to see the area since 1540.

In August of the same year, two priests, of the Order of Friars Minor, Francisco Atanasio Domínguez and Francisco Silvestre Vélez de Escalante, with a small party and a pack train, started northward from Santa Fé, following the trappers' and traders' trail to the left-bank tributaries of the Colorado. Their aim was to find a route to Monterey, California, by circumventing the Canyon Country on the north. They also hoped to find sites for missions and settlements among the Indians of the region. They crossed the Colorado in Grand Valley and discovered the Green River, naming it the *San Buenaventura*. The party then turned west across the Wasatch Plateau to Utah Lake, thence south along the high plateaus which form the boundary between the Great Basin and the Colorado Plateau. But by this time winter was approaching, so near the site of present-day St. George, Utah, Domínguez and Escalante finally abandoned hope of reaching California and turned southeast. They reached the Colorado at Lee's Ferry but could not cross there. They turned east, scaling the Vermilion Cliffs, and finally found a crossing at a point they called *La Purísima Concepción de la Virgen Santísima,* now called Crossing of the Fathers in their honor.

The explorations of Domínquez and Escalante made the Canyon Country known to the officialdom of New Spain. Escalante had kept a meticulous diary of the journey, noting many details of the country, the flora and fauna, and the Indians. Accompanying the party was Bernardo de Miera y Pacheco, a cartographer. Miera made several excellent multicolored maps showing land forms, the route of travel, territories of Indian tribes, and other valuable information. The maps do contain errors, principally in country not visited by the party. Utah Lake and the Great Salt Lake are shown as one body of water with an outlet to the Pacific Ocean. The *San Buenaventura* (Green River) is shown as flowing west into Sevier Lake. But despite these errors, Miera's maps were of great value. They and Escalante's diary were forwarded to the Viceroy of New Spain and, ultimately, to the King of Spain.

Information from Miera's maps was used, indirectly, by Alexander von Humboldt for the maps which accompanied his *Political Essay on the Kingdom of New Spain* (4-volume English edition, published 1811). The wide circulation of Humboldt's work made a map of the Canyon Country generally available, albeit one which perpetuated Miera's errors.

Although Domínguez and Escalante failed to reach California, they discovered large sections of what was soon to become the Old Spanish Trail. The trail ran northwestward from Santa Fé to cross the Colorado at the site of present-day Moab, Utah, north to the Green at the site of Green River, Utah, then west along the Book Cliffs to the Wasatch Plateau. There were several routes across the plateau to Utah Lake or to the Sevier Valley. The trail then turned southwestward to San Gabriel, California. From before 1820 until the 1850's, Spanish, Mexican, Indian, and White traders and trappers traveled the trail from Santa Fé to California. The traders dealt in furs, woolen goods, horses, mules, and sometimes slaves—Paiute, Gosiute, and Shoshoni Indians captured and carried to Santa Fé or California.

The Old Spanish Trail circumvented the deeply dissected terrain which is the heart of the Canyon Country. The area was largely left to the Utes and Southern Paiutes. Few caravans followed the Crossing of the Fathers trail northwestward from Santa Fé, although the trader Antonio Armijo with a party of thirty men did so in 1829.

The advent of the American fur trade in the 1820's brought hundreds of "Mountain Men" onto the headwaters of the Green River and into the Uinta Basin. Most of the trappers skirted the Canyon Country, remaining in the upper Green River area. If they did venture south they followed the Spanish Trail. Jedediah Smith and others passed along the trail and along the lower Colorado in the 1820's but they did not venture into the Canyon Country. In 1826 a party of trappers, of which James Ohio Pattie was a member, apparently ascended the lower Colorado to the Virgin River and then turned eastward, ultimately arriving in Santa Fé. Unfortunately, Pattie's diary of the trip is so vague that it is not even clear whether the party moved along the north or the south rim of the Grand Canyon.

A few trappers did explore the area south of the Uinta Basin. Some of the men who worked for Antoine Roubidoux, who had established a post in the Uinta Basin in 1831 or 1832, may have done so, but there are no records to substantiate their travels.

A man who may have worked for Roubidoux, one Denis Julien, apparently explored as far south as Cataract Canyon. His name and the date "1836" are found inscribed on the walls of Labyrinth and Still-water canyons on the Green and in Cataract Canyon on the Colorado. Julien may have traveled by boat, but again there is no documentation.

But though some few trappers explored into the heart of the Canyon Country, their knowledge of the area was not made public. As late as 1844, the relationship of the Green and the Colorado remained uncertain. Finally in that year Captain John C. Frémont finally laid the matter to rest. He had traversed, and named, the Great Basin and had understood its true physiography, that it had no outlet to the sea. He saw that Miera's westward-flowing *San Buenaventura* and the outlet for the Great Salt Lake were myths. The maps in Frémont's reports, drawn by Charles Preuss, show the Green as an affluent of the Colorado (although the confluence is shown too far south). Beyond the confluence, the country is marked "Unexplored."

The end of the Mexican War in 1847 saw the beginnings of increased exploration of the Canyon Country by the United States Army. These expeditions had various purposes—surveys of wagon roads, Indian pacification, and, in the 1850's, surveys of possible routes for the proposed transcontinental railroad.

One such party was led by Captain James W. Gunnison in 1853. The Gunnison party passed through central Colorado and crossed both the Grand and Green rivers.

Redbud Canyon on the San Juan River—two miles below this spot is Music Temple of Glen Canyon (now flooded) where Powell's party camped. Names of the three men who later deserted Powell were carved in a rock near the grotto's entrance.

There was also the question of whether the Colorado River was navigable. By the early 1850's there were steamboats operating on the lower river, from the mouth to Fort Mohave. In 1857 Lt. Joseph Christmas Ives, with a party of men, ascended the lower Colorado in a 54-foot steamboat, as far as Black Canyon, the site of Hoover Dam. At that point the party left the river and traveled overland, exploring the floor of the Grand Canyon, the first recorded instance. The significance of this expedition is increased by the presence of Dr. John Strong Newberry. For the first time a trained geologist saw and described the geological complexities of the Grand Canyon.

Newberry remained in the West and in 1859 accompanied Captain John M. Macomb from Santa Fé to the junction of the Grand and the Green rivers. Again, Newberry was the first scientist to see and describe that area. His observations firmly resolved the question of the relation of the Green and the Colorado and confirmed Frémont's map. Newberry's reports on these trips remain as early scientific classics.

At about the same time, Jacob Hamblin, the famed Mormon explorer and missionary to the Indians, was probing the Canyon Country. Between 1858 and 1869 Hamblin led seven expeditions from southern Utah across the Colorado into Hopi and Navajo country to missionize, explore, and, sometimes, keep the peace. In the course of these activities Hamblin and his men crossed and recrossed the Colorado at various points and circled the perimeter of the Grand Canyon.

In 1869 Hamblin and others founded the settlement of Kanab in southern Utah. In the fall of 1870 Powell accompanied Hamblin, Brigham Young, John D. Lee (soon to be excommunicated for his alleged part in the 1858 Mountain Meadows Massacre and to go into hiding at Lonely Dell where he would be of help to Powell and his men on their second river trip), and others from Salt Lake City to Kanab where Young officially dedicated the townsite.

Powell and his men used Kanab as a base camp from 1871 through 1874. Hamblin also accompanied Powell to the Uinkarets Plateau in the fall of 1870 and helped him make peace with the Indians who had killed Dunn and the Howland brothers the previous year. Hamblin and some of his men worked for Powell in 1871–72, packing supplies to the river parties.

III

Thus, by January of 1869 when Powell was scouting the Green River and deciding to make his river trip, White men had been exploring and learning about the Colorado River and the Canyon Country for nearly 330 years, and the Indians for at least four times that long. Well-worn trails circumvented the country, crossing it and its rivers only at certain points. By 1869 the general relationship of the Green and Colorado were, at last, clear. But the rivers themselves and most of their tributaries were not known, nor was much of the country away from the trails, especially south of the Uinta Basin. The spectacular buttes and mesas, and the deep, often "sawcut" lateral canyons were (and are) serious barriers to travel and exploration. Indeed, some parts of the country were yet totally unknown to White men. Powell and his men were to discover a mountain range, the Henrys, and a river, the Escalante, in the course of their explorations.

Powell and his men proved equal to the task of exploring, and describing, the Canyon Country—rumors of giant whirlpools and sinking rivers notwithstanding.

Powell's articles on the Canyon Country in *Scribner's Monthly* in 1874–75, and his 1875 report, *Explorations of the Colorado River of the West and Its Tributaries . . .* , created a sensation when they appeared.

The second section of the report, "On the Physical Features of the Valley of the Colorado," is a remarkably lucid, sober, and concise discussion of the geology of the Canyon Country. A number of geological concepts advanced therein to explain the formation of the country, its canyons and mountains, remain in current use.

The first part of the report, the narrative or diary section, is a compilation of Powell's journals of both river trips, some newspaper articles he had written during the first trip, and the *Scribner's* articles. The narrative is written *as if* everything chronicled therein occurred during the first trip. Events which actually occurred in 1871 and 1872 are reported as happening in 1869. There is no mention of the personnel of the 1871–72 party, nor is there an indication that there even *was* a second trip. The engravings illustrating the report were made from photographs taken by Beaman and Hillers between 1871 and 1874, but this fact is not noted.

This "telescoping" of events has created a sense of righteous indignation in the breasts of historians and other clock-watchers ever since. But Powell seems never to have intended the narrative as a historical record. He was engaged in public relations, attempting to excite the interest and attention of the public and the United States Congress,

John Wesley Powell
Diary of the First Trip
Through the Grand Canyon
1869

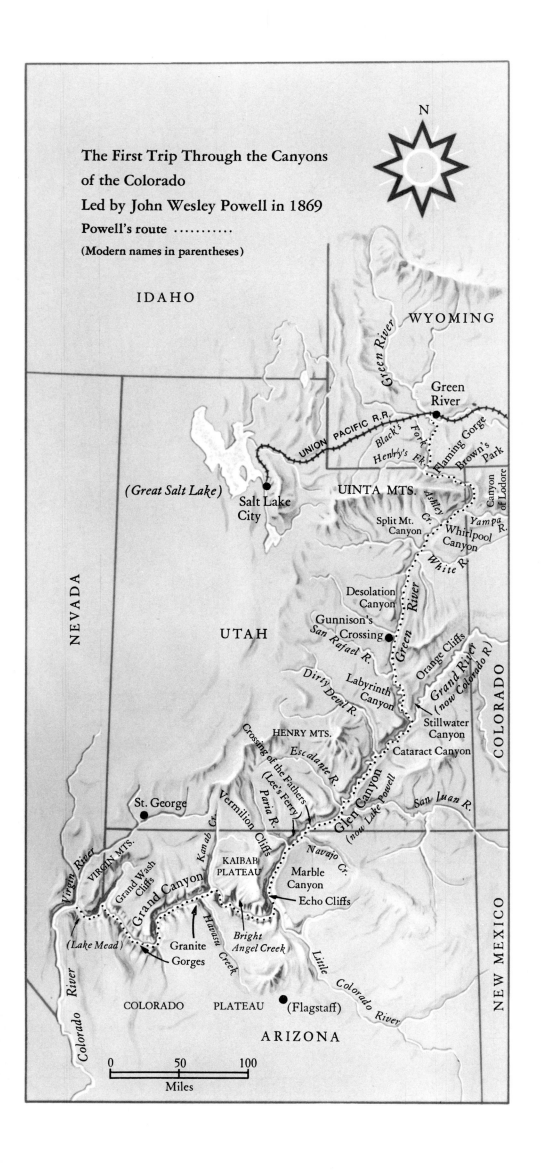

**The First Trip Through the Canyons
of the Colorado
Led by John Wesley Powell in 1869**

Powell's route ...........

(Modern names in parentheses)

IDAHO

WYOMING

*Green River*

Green
River

UNION PACIFIC R.R.

*Black's Fork*

*Henry's Fk.*

*Flaming Gorge*

*Brown's Park*

(Great Salt Lake)

Salt Lake
City

UINTA MTS.

*Ashley Cr.*

Split Mt.
Canyon

Whirlpool
Canyon

*Yampa R.*

Canyon
of Lodore

NEVADA

UTAH

*White R.*

Desolation
Canyon

Gunnison's
Crossing

*San Rafael R.*

*Green River*

Orange Cliffs

*Grand River
(now Colorado R.)*

COLORADO

*Dirty Devil R.*

Labyrinth
Canyon

HENRY MTS.

*Escalante R.*

Stillwater
Canyon

Cataract Canyon

Crossing of the Fathers

(Lee's Ferry)

*Paria R.*

St. George

*Vermilion Cliffs*

*Kanab Cr.*

Glen Canyon
(now Lake Powell)

*San Juan R.*

*Navajo Cr.*

KAIBAB
PLATEAU

Marble
Canyon

Echo Cliffs

*Virgin River*

VIRGIN MTS.

*Grand Wash Cliffs*

Grand Canyon

*Havasu Creek*

*Bright
Angel Creek*

(Lake Mead)

Granite
Gorges

*Little
Colorado River*

NEW MEXICO

*Colorado River*

COLORADO    PLATEAU    (Flagstaff)

ARIZONA

0     50     100
Miles

# From Green River City
# to Flaming Gorge

May 24, 1869.

The good people of Green River City, Wyoming, turn out to see us start. We raise our little flag, push the boats from shore, and the swift current carries us down.

Our boats are four in number.* Three are built of oak; stanch and firm; doubled-ribbed, with double stem and stern posts, and further strengthened by bulkheads, dividing each into three compartments.

Two of these, the fore and aft, are decked, forming water-tight cabins. It is expected these will buoy the boats should the waves roll over them in rough water. The little vessels are twenty-one feet long, and, taking out the cargoes, can be carried by four men.

The fourth boat is made of pine, very light, but sixteen feet in length, with a sharp cut-water, and every way built for fast rowing, and divided into compartments as the others.

We take with us rations deemed sufficient to last ten months; for we expect, when winter comes on and the river is filled with ice, to lie over at some point until spring arrives; so we take with us abundant supplies of clothing. We have also a large quantity of ammunition and two or three dozen traps. For the purpose of building cabins, repairing boats, and meeting other exigencies, we are supplied with axes, hammers, saws, augers, and other tools, and a quantity of nails and screws. For scientific work, we have two sextants, four chronometers, a number of barometers, thermometers, compasses, and other instruments.

The flour is divided into three equal parts; the meat and all other articles of our rations in the same way. Each of the larger boats has an ax, hammer, saw, auger, and other tools, so that all are loaded alike. We distribute the cargoes in this way, that we may not be entirely destitute of some important article should any one of the boats be lost. In the small boat, we pack a part of the scientific instruments, three

The start at Green River.

One-armed Major Powell with Second River Party in 1871. There was no photographer on the first trip.

* Boats were built in Chicago and transported by rail to the point where the Union Pacific Railroad crosses the Green River. With these we were to descend the Green into the Colorado, and the Colorado down to the foot of the Grand Canyon.

guns, and three small bundles of clothing only. In this, I proceed in advance, to explore the channel.

J. C. Sumner and William H. Dunn are my boatmen in the *Emma Dean*; then follows *Kitty Clyde's Sister,* manned by W. H. Powell and G. Y. Bradley; next, the *No Name,* with O. G. Howland, Seneca Howland, and Frank Goodman; and last comes the *Maid of the Canyon,* with W. R. Hawkins and Andrew Hall.

Sumner was a soldier during the late war, and before and since that time has been a great traveler in the wilds of the Mississippi Valley and the Rocky Mountains as an amateur hunter. He is a fair-haired, delicate-looking man, but a veteran in experience, and has performed the feat of crossing the Rocky Mountains in midwinter on snowshoes. He spent the winter of 1886–87 in Middle Park, Colorado, for the purpose of making some natural history collections for me, and succeeded in killing three grizzlies, two mountain lions, and a large number of elk, deer, sheep, wolves, beavers, and many other animals. When Bayard Taylor traveled through the parks of Colorado, Sumner was his guide, and he speaks in glowing terms of Mr. Taylor's genial qualities in camp, but he was mortally offended when the great traveler requested him to act as doorkeeper at Breckenridge to receive the admission fee from those who attended his lectures.

Dunn was a hunter, trapper, and mule-packer in Colorado for many years. He dresses in buckskin with a dark oleaginous luster, doubtless due to the fact that he has lived on fat venison and killed many beavers since he first donned his uniform years ago. His raven hair falls down to his back, for he has a sublime contempt of shears and razors.

Captain Powell was an officer of artillery during the late war and was captured on the 22nd day of July, 1864, at Atlanta and served a ten months' term in prison at Charleston, where he was placed with other officers under fire. He is silent, moody, and sarcastic, though sometimes he enlivens the camp at night with a song. He is never surprised at anything, his coolness never deserts him, and he would choke the belching throat of a volcano if he thought the spitfire meant anything but fun. We call him "Old Shady."

Bradley, a lieutenant during the late war, and since orderly sergeant in the regular army, was, a few weeks previous to our start, discharged, by order of the Secretary of War, that he might go on this trip. He is scrupulously careful, and a little mishap works him into a passion, but when labor is needed he has a ready hand and powerful arm, and

This pool at Seven-Mile Canyon and the entire side canyon were flooded when the Colorado was dammed at Glen Canyon in 1963.

A valley west of Green River.

The high plateaus.

in danger, rapid judgment and unerring skill. A great difficulty or peril changes the petulant spirit into a brave, generous soul.

O. G. Howland is a printer by trade, an editor by profession, and a hunter by choice. When busily employed he usually puts his hat in his pocket, and his thin hair and long beard stream in the wind, giving him a wild look, much like that of King Lear in an illustrated copy of Shakespeare which tumbles around the camp.

Seneca Howland is a quiet, pensive young man, and a great favorite with all.

Goodman is a stranger to us—a stout, willing Englishman, with florid face and more florid anticipations of a glorious trip.

Billy Hawkins, the cook, was a soldier in the Union Army during the war, and when discharged at its close went West, and since then has been engaged as teamster on the plains or hunter in the mountains. He is an athlete and a jovial good fellow, who hardly seems to know his own strength.

Hall is a Scotch boy, nineteen years old, with what seems to us a "secondhand head," which doubtless came down to him from some knight who wore it during the Border Wars. It looks a very old head indeed, with deep-set blue eyes and beaked nose. Young as he is, Hall has had experience in hunting, trapping, and fighting Indians, and he makes the most of it, for he can tell a good story, and is never encumbered by unnecessary scruples in giving to his narratives those embellishments which help to make a story complete. He is always ready for work or play and is a good hand at either.

Davis Gulch on the Escalante River near Lake Powell.

Our boats are heavily loaded, and only with the utmost care is it possible to float in the rough river without shipping water.

A mile or two below town, we run on a sand bar. The men jump into the stream, and thus lighten the vessels, so that they drift over; and on we go. In trying to avoid a rock, an oar is broken on one of the boats, and, thus crippled, she strikes. The current is swift, and she is sent reeling and rocking into the eddy. In the confusion, two others are lost overboard and the men seem quite discomfited, much to the amusement of the other members of the party.

Catching the oars and starting again, the boats are once more borne down the stream until we land at a small cottonwood grove on the bank, and camp for noon.

During the afternoon, we run down to a point where the river sweeps the foot of an overhanging cliff, and here we camp for the night. The sun is yet two hours high, so I climb the cliffs, and walk back among the strangely carved rocks of the Green River badlands. These are sandstones and shales, gray and buff, red and brown, blue and black strata in many alternations, lying nearly horizontal, and almost without soil and vegetation. They are very friable, and the rain and streams have carved them into quaint shapes. Barren desolation is stretched before me; and yet there is a beauty in the scene. The fantastic carving, imitating architectural forms, and suggesting rude but weird statuary, with the bright and varied colors of the rocks, conspire to make a scene such as the dweller in verdure-clad hills can scarcely appreciate.

Standing on a high point, I can look off in every direction over a vast landscape, with salient rocks and cliffs glittering in the evening sun. Dark shadows are settling in the valleys and gulches, and the heights are made higher and the depths deeper by the glamour and witchery of light and shade.

Away to the south, the Uinta Mountains stretch in a long line; high peaks thrust into the sky, and snow fields glittering like lakes of molten silver; and pine forests in somber green; and rosy clouds playing around the borders of huge, black masses; and heights and clouds, and mountains and snow fields, and forests and rock-lands, are blended into one grand view. Now the sun goes down, and I return to camp.

## May 25.

We start early this morning, and run along at a good rate until about nine o'clock, when we are brought up on a gravelly bar. All jump out,

Badlands.

and help the boats over by main strength. Then a rain comes on, and river and clouds conspire to give us a thorough drenching. Wet, chilled, and tired to exhaustion, we stop at a cottonwood grove on the bank, build a huge fire, make a cup of coffee, and are soon refreshed and quite merry. When the clouds "get out of our sunshine," we start again. A few miles farther down, a flock of mountain sheep are seen on a cliff to the right. The boats are quietly tied up, and three or four men go after them. In the course of two or three hours, they return. The cook has been successful in bringing down a fat lamb. The unsuccessful hunters taunt him with finding it dead; but it is soon dressed, cooked, and eaten, making a fine four o'clock dinner.

"All aboard," and down the river for another dozen miles. On the way, we pass the mouth of Black's Fork, a dirty little stream that seems somewhat swollen. Just below its mouth, we land and camp.

May 26.

Today, we pass several curiously shaped buttes, standing between the west bank of the river and the high bluffs beyond. These buttes are outliers of the same beds of rocks exposed on the faces of the bluffs; thinly laminated shales and sandstones of many colors, standing above in vertical cliffs, and buttressed below with a water-carved talus; some of them attain an altitude of nearly a thousand feet above the level of the river.

We glide quietly down the placid stream past the carved cliffs of the *mauvaises terres,* now and then obtaining glimpses of distant mountains. Occasionally, deer are started from the glades among the willows; and several wild geese, after a chase through the water, are shot. . . .

Two or three miles below, Henry's Fork enters from the right. We land a short distance above the junction, where a cache of instruments and rations was made several months ago, in a cave at the foot of the cliff, a distance back from the river. Here it was safe from the elements and wild beasts, but not from man. Some anxiety is felt, as we have learned that a party of Indians have been camped near it for several weeks. Our fears are soon allayed, for we find it all right. Our chronometer wheels are not taken for hair ornaments; our barometer tubes, for beads; nor the sextant thrown into the river as "bad medicine," as had been predicted.

Taking up our cache, we pass down to the foot of the Uinta Mountains, and, in a cold storm, go into camp.

These boats of the second expedition were almost exactly the same as those used by Powell in 1869. Rubber bags that could withstand soaking kept most of the provisions dry on the second trip.

The river is running to the south; the mountains have an easterly and westerly trend directly athwart its course, yet it glides on in a quiet way as if it thought a mountain range no formidable obstruction to its course. It enters the range by a flaring, brilliant, red gorge, that may be seen from the north a score of miles away.

The great mass of the mountain ridge through which the gorge is cut is composed of bright vermilion rocks; but they are surmounted by broad bands of mottled buff and gray, and these bands come down with a gentle curve to the water's edge on the nearer slope of the mountain.

This is the head of the first canyon we are about to explore—an introductory one to a series made by the river through this range. We name it Flaming Gorge. The cliffs or walls we find, on measurement, to be about one thousand two hundred feet high.

Camp at Flaming Gorge.

## May 27.

Today it rains, and we employ the time in repairing one of our barometers, which was broken on the way from New York. A new tube has to be put in; that is, a long glass tube has to be filled with mercury four or five inches at a time, and each installment boiled over a spirit-lamp. It is a delicate task to do this without breaking the glass; but we have success, and are ready to measure mountains once more.

## May 28.

Today we go to the summit of the cliff on the left and take observations for altitude, and are variously employed in topographic and geological work.

## May 29.

This morning, Bradley and I cross the river, and climb more than a thousand feet to a point where we can see the stream sweeping in a long, beautiful curve through the gorge below. Turning and looking to the west, we can see the valley of Henry's Fork, through which, for many miles, the little river flows in a tortuous channel.* . . .

For many years, this valley has been the home of a number of mountaineers, who were originally hunters and trappers, living with the Indians. Most of them have one or more Indian wives. They no longer roam with the nomadic tribes in pursuit of buckskin or beaver,

* Other diaries suggest this occurred on the second expedition, May 30, 1871; Hillers, not Bradley, was Major Powell's companion.

Primroses such as these on a sand dune near Hidden Passage were a familiar sight before the flooding of Glen Canyon.

but have accumulated herds of cattle and horses, and consider themselves quite well-to-do. Some of them have built cabins; others still live in lodges.

John Baker is one of the most famous of these men; and, from our point of view, we can see his lodge three or four miles up the river. . . .

# From Flaming Gorge
# to the Gate of Lodore

You must not think of a mountain range as a line of peaks standing on a plain, but as a broad platform many miles wide, from which mountains have been carved by the waters. You must conceive, too, that this plateau is cut by gulches and canyons in many directions, and that beautiful valleys are scattered about at different altitudes. The first series of canyons we are about to explore constitutes a river channel through such a range of mountains. The canyon is cut nearly halfway through the range, then turns to the east, and is cut along the central line, or axis, gradually crossing it to the south. Keeping this direction for more than fifty miles, it then turns abruptly to a southwest course, and goes diagonally through the southern slope of the range. . . .

May 30.
This morning we are ready to enter the mysterious canyon, and start with some anxiety. The old mountaineers tell us that it cannot be run; the Indians say, "Water heap catch 'em," but all are eager for the trial, and off we go.

Entering Flaming Gorge, we quickly run through it on a swift current, and emerge into a little park. Half a mile below, the river wheels sharply to the left, and we turned into another canyon cut into the mountain. We enter the narrow passage. On either side the walls rapidly increase in altitude. On the left are overhanging ledges and cliffs five hundred—a thousand—fifteen hundred feet high.

On the right, the rocks are broken and ragged, and the water fills the channel from cliff to cliff. Now the river turns abruptly around a point to the right, and the waters plunge swiftly down among great rocks; and here we have our first experience with canyon rapids. I stand up on the deck of my boat to seek a way among the wave-beaten rocks. All untried as we are with such waters, the moments are filled with intense anxiety. Soon our boats reach the swift current; a stroke or two, now on this side, now on that, and we thread the narrow passage with exhilarating velocity, mounting the high waves, whose foaming crests dash over us, and plunging into the troughs, until we reach the quiet water below; and then comes a feeling of great relief. Our first rapid is run. Another mile, and we come into the valley again.

Let me explain this canyon. Where the river turns to the left above, it takes a course directly into the mountain, penetrating to its very heart, then wheels back upon itself, and runs out into the valley from which it started only half a mile below the point at which it entered; so the canyon is in the form of an elongated letter U, with the apex in the center of the mountain. We name it Horseshoe Canyon.

Soon we leave the valley, and enter another short canyon, very narrow at first, but widening below as the canyon walls increase in height. Here we discover the mouth of a beautiful little creek, coming down through its narrow water-worn cleft. Just at its entrance there is a park of two or three hundred acres, walled on every side by almost vertical cliffs, hundreds of feet in altitude, with three gateways through the walls—one up, another down the river, and a third passage through which the creek comes in. The river is broad, deep, and quiet, and its waters mirror towering rocks.

Kingfishers are playing about the streams, and so we adopt as names Kingfisher Creek, Kingfisher Park, and Kingfisher Canyon. At night, we camp at the foot of this canyon. . . .

May 31.
We start down another canyon, and reach rapids made dangerous by high rocks lying in the channel; so we run ashore, and let our boats down with lines. In the afternoon we come to more dangerous rapids, and stop to examine them. I find we must do the same work again, but, being on the wrong side of the river to obtain a foothold, must first cross over—no very easy matter in such a current, with

Horseshoe Canyon.

rapids and rocks below. We take the pioneer boat *Emma Dean* over, and unload her on the bank; then she returns and takes another load. Running back and forth, she soon has half our cargo over; then one of the larger boats is manned and taken across, but carried down almost to the rocks in spite of hard rowing. The other boats follow and make the landing, and we go into camp for the night. . . .

As the twilight deepens, the rocks grow dark and somber; the threatening roar of the water is loud and constant, and I lie awake with thoughts of the morrow and the canyons to come, interrupted now and then by characteristics of the scenery that attract my attention. And here I make a discovery. On looking at the mountain directly in front, the steepness of the slope is greatly exaggerated, while the distance to its summit and its true altitude are correspondingly diminished. I have heretofore found that to properly judge of the slope of a mountainside, you must see it in profile. In coming down the river this afternoon, I observed the slope of a particular part of the wall, and made an estimate of its altitude. While at supper, I noticed the same cliff from a position facing it, and it seemed steeper, but not half as high. Now lying on my side and looking at it, the true proportions appear. This seems a wonder, and I rise up to take a view of it standing. It is the same cliff as at supper time. Lying down again, it is the cliff as seen in profile, with a long slope and distant summit. Musing on this, I forget "the morrow and the canyons to come." I find a way to estimate the altitude and slope of an inclination as I can judge of distance along the horizon. The reason is simple. A reference to the stereoscope will suggest it. The distance between the eyes forms a base-line for optical triangulation.

June 1.

Today we have an exciting ride. The river rolls down the canyon at a wonderful rate, and, with no rocks in the way, we make almost railroad speed. Here and there the water rushes into a narrow gorge; the rocks on the side roll it into the center in great waves, and the boats go leaping and bounding over these like things of life. They remind me of scenes witnessed in Middle Park; herds of startled deer bounding through forests beset with fallen timber. I mention the resemblance to some of the hunters, and so striking is it that it comes to be a common expression, "See the black tails jumping

Near this sculptured rock at House Rock Rapids the second Powell expedition left the river in November 1871 for the winter's campaign in the Kanab Region.

the logs." At times the waves break and roll over the boats, which necessitates much bailing, and obliges us to stop occasionally for that purpose.

June 2.

This morning we make a trail among the rocks, transport the cargoes to a point below the falls, let the remaining boats over and are ready to start before noon.

On a high rock by which the trail passes we find the inscription: "Ashley 18–5." The third figure is obscure—some of the party reading it 1835, some 1855.

James Baker, an old-time mountaineer, once told me about a party of men starting down the river, and Ashley was named as one. The story runs that the boat was swamped, and some of the party drowned in one of the canyons below. The word "Ashley" is a warning to us, and we resolve on great caution.

Ashley Falls is the name we give to the cataract.

The river is very narrow; the right wall vertical for two or three hundred feet, the left towering to a great height, with a vast pile of broken rocks lying between the foot of the cliff and the water. Some of the rocks broken down from the ledge above have tumbled into the channel and caused this fall. One great cubical block, thirty or forty feet high, stands in the middle of the stream, and the waters, parting to either side, plunge down about twelve feet, and are broken again by the smaller rocks into a rapid below. Immediately below the falls, the water occupies the entire channel, there being no talus at the foot of the cliffs. . . .

Boats of the second expedition after the portage of Ashley Falls.

June 3.

This morning we spread our rations, clothes, &c., on the ground to dry, and several of the party go out for a hunt. I take a walk of five or six miles up to a pine grove park, its grassy carpet bedecked with crimson, velvet flowers, set in groups on the stems of pear-shaped cactus plants; patches of painted cups are seen here and there, with yellow blossoms protruding through scarlet bracts; little blue-eyed flowers are peeping through the grass; and the air is filled with fragrance from the white blossoms of a *Spiræa*. A mountain brook runs through the midst, ponded below by beaver dams. It is a quiet place for retirement from the raging waters of the canyon. . . .

The little valleys above are beautiful parks; between the parks are stately pine forests, half hiding ledges of red sandstone. Mule-deer and elk abound; grizzly bears, too, are abundant; wild cats, wolverines, and mountain lions are here at home. The forest aisles are filled with the music of birds, and the parks are decked with flowers. Noisy brooks meander through them; ledges of moss-covered rocks are seen; and gleaming in the distance are the snow fields, and the mountain tops are away in the clouds.

June 4.

We start early and run through to Brown's Park. Halfway down the valley, a spur of a red mountain stretches across the river, which cuts a canyon through it. Here the walls are comparatively low, but vertical. A vast number of swallows have built their adobe houses on the face of the cliffs, on either side of the river. The waters are deep and quiet, but the swallows are swift and noisy enough, sweeping by in their curved paths through the air, or chattering from the rocks. The young birds stretch their little heads on naked necks through the doorways of their mud houses, clamoring for food. They are a noisy people.

We call this Swallow Canyon.

June 5.

With one of the men, I climb a mountain, off on the right. A long spur, with broken ledges of rock, puts down to the river; and along its course, or up the "hogback," as it is called, I make the ascent. Dunn, who is climbing to the same point, is coming up the gulch. Two hours' hard work has brought us to the summit. These mountains are all verdure clad; pine and cedar forests are set on green terraces; snow-clad mountains are seen in the distance, to the west; the plains of the upper Green stretch out before us, to the north, until they are lost in the blue heavens; but half of the river-cleft range intervenes, and the river itself is at our feet. . . .

Hogbacks.

To the east, we look up the valley of the Vermilion, through which Frémont found his path on his way to the great parks of Colorado.

June 6.

At daybreak, I am awakened by a chorus of birds. It seems as if all the feathered songsters of the region have come to the old tree. Several species of warblers, woodpeckers, and flickers above, meadowlarks in the grass, and wild geese in the river. I recline on my elbow, and watch a lark near by, and then awaken my bed fellow, to listen to my Jenny Lind. A morning concert for me; none of your *"matinées."*

Our cook has been an ox-driver, or "bull-whacker," on the plains, in one of those long trains now no longer seen, and he hasn't forgotten his old ways. In the midst of the concert, his voice breaks in: "Roll out! roll out! bulls in the corral! chain up the gaps! Roll out! roll out! roll out!" And this is our breakfast bell.

June 7.

Today, two or three of us climb to the summit of the cliff, on the left, and find its altitude, above camp, to be 2,086 feet. The rocks are split with fissures, deep and narrow, sometimes a hundred feet, or more, to the bottom. Lofty pines find root in the fissures that are filled with loose earth and decayed vegetation. On a rock we find a pool of clear, cold water, caught from yesterday evening's shower. After a good drink, we walk out to the brink of the canyon, and look down to the water below. I can do this now, but it has taken several years of mountain climbing to cool my nerves, so that I can sit, with my feet over the edge, and calmly look down a precipice 2,000 feet. And yet I cannot look on and see another do the same. I must either bid him come away, or turn my head. . . .

Members of the second expedition pose near the Green River.

# The Canyon of Lodore

June 8.

We enter the canyon, and, until noon, find a succession of rapids, over which our boats have to be taken.

Here I must explain our method of proceeding at such places. The *Emma Dean* goes in advance; the other boats follow, in obedience to signals. When we approach a rapid, or what, on other rivers, would often be called a fall, I stand on deck to examine it, while the oarsmen back water, and we drift on as slowly as possible. If I can see a clear chute between the rocks, away we go; but if the channel is beset entirely across, we signal the other boats, pull to land, and I walk along the shore for closer examination. If this reveals no clear

Cliff with tumbleweed at House Rock Canyon.

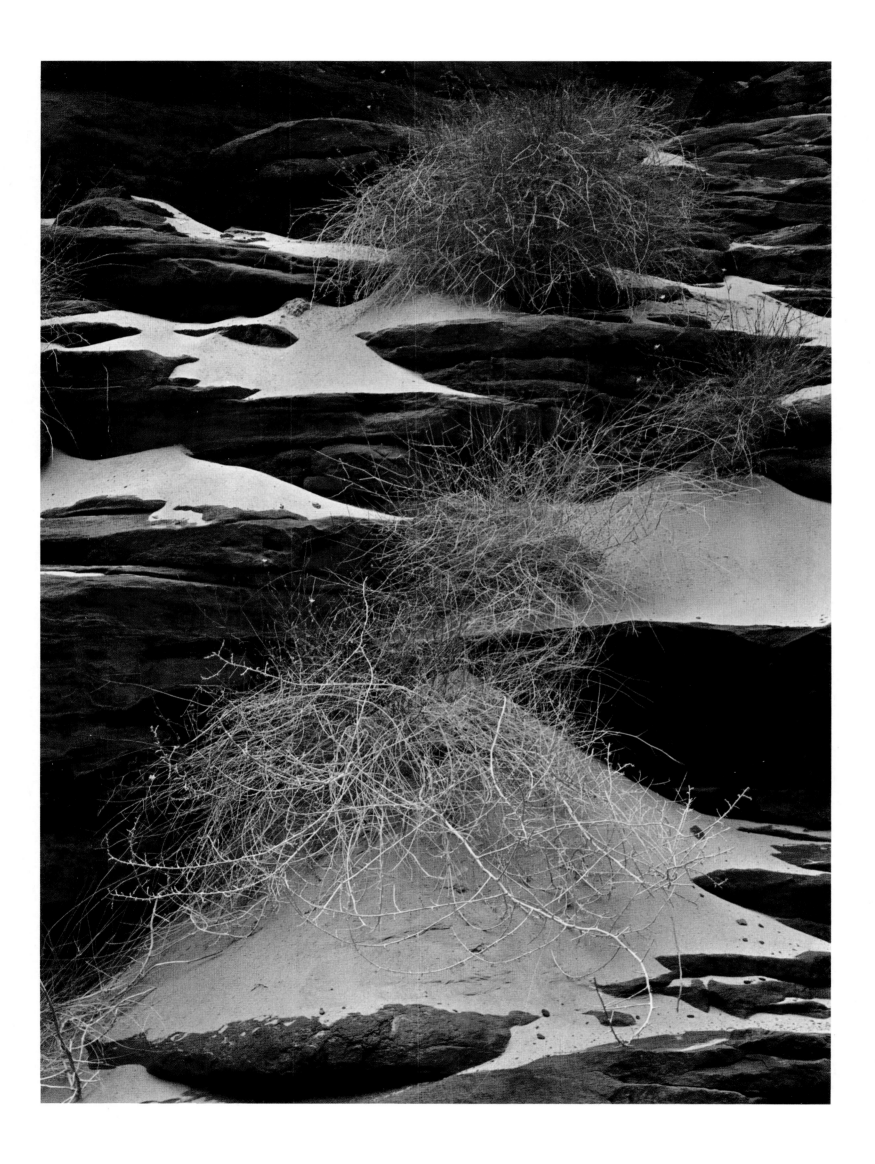

channel, hard work begins. We drop the boats to the very head of the dangerous place, and let them over by lines, or make a portage, frequently carrying both boats and cargoes over the rocks, or, perhaps, only the cargoes, if it is safe to let the boats down.

The waves caused by such falls in a river differ much from the waves of the sea. The water of an ocean wave merely rises and falls; the form only passes on, and form chases form unceasingly. A body floating on such waves merely rises and sinks—does not progress unless impelled by wind or some other power. But here, the water of the wave passes on, while the form remains. The waters plunge down ten or twenty feet, to the foot of a fall; spring up again in a great wave; then down and up, in a series of billows, that gradually disappear in the more quiet waters below; but these waves are always there, and you can stand above and count them.

Canyon of Lodore, or as the men referred to it, "Hell's Half Mile."

A boat riding such, leaps and plunges along with great velocity. Now, the difficulty in riding over these falls, when the rocks are out of the way, is in the first wave at the foot. This will sometimes gather for a moment, heaping up higher and higher, until it breaks back. If the boat strikes it the instant after it breaks, she cuts through, and the mad breaker dashes its spray over the boat, and would wash us overboard did we not cling tight. If the boat, in going over the falls, chances to get caught in some side current, and is turned from its course, so as to strike the wave "broadside on," and the wave breaks at the same instant, the boat is capsized. Still, we must cling to her, for, the watertight compartments acting as buoys, she cannot sink; and so we go, dragged through the waves, until still waters are reached. We then right the boat, and climb aboard. We have several such experiences today.

At night, we camp on the right bank, on a little shelving rock, between the river and the foot of the cliff; and with night comes gloom into these great depths.

After supper, we sit by our campfire, made of driftwood caught by the rocks, and tell stories of wild life; for the men have seen such in the mountains, or on the plains, and on the battlefields of the South. It is late before we spread our blankets on the beach. . . .

June 9.
One of the party suggests that we call this the Canyon of Lodore, and the name is adopted. Very slowly we make our way, often climbing

on the rocks at the edge of the water for a few hundred yards, to examine the channel before running it.

During the afternoon, we come to a place where it is necessary to make a portage. The little boat is landed, and the others are signaled to come up.

When these rapids or broken falls occur, usually the channel is suddenly narrowed by rocks which have been tumbled from the the cliffs or have been washed in by lateral streams. Immediately above the narrow, rocky channel, on one or both sides, there is often a bay of quiet water, in which we can land with ease. Sometimes the water descends with a smooth, unruffled surface, from the broad, quiet spread above, into the narrow, angry channel below, by a semicircular sag. Great care must be taken not to pass over the brink into this deceptive pit, but above it we can row with safety. I walk along the bank to examine the ground, leaving one of my men with a flag to guide the other boats to the landing-place. I soon see one of the boats make shore all right and feel no more concern; but a minute after, I hear a shout, and looking around, see one of the boats shooting down the center of the sag. It is the *No Name,* with Captain Howland, his brother, and Goodman. I feel that its going over is inevitable, and run to save the third boat. A minute more, and she turns the point and heads for the shore. Then I turn down stream again, and scramble along to look for the boat that has gone over. The first fall is not great, only ten or twelve feet, and we often run such; but below, the river tumbles down again for forty or fifty feet, in a channel filled with dangerous rocks that break the waves into whirlpools and beat them into foam. I pass around a great crag just in time to see the boat strike a rock, and, rebounding from the shock, careen and fill the open compartment with water. Two of the men lose their oars; she swings around, and is carried down at a rapid rate, broadside on, for a few yards, and strikes amidships on another rock with great force, is broken quite in two, and the men are thrown into the river; the larger part of the boat floating buoyantly, they soon seize it, and down the river they drift, past the rocks for a few hundred yards to a second rapid, filled with huge boulders, where the boat strikes again, and is dashed to pieces, and the men and fragments are soon carried beyond my sight. Running along, I turn a bend, and see a man's head above the water, washed about in a whirlpool below a great rock.

It is Frank Goodman, clinging to it with a grip upon which life

Near the boat is Major Powell's chair, which was strapped on top of the *Emma Dean* at midships to give the one-armed leader a view of the unknown river downstream.

depends. Coming opposite, I see Howland trying to go to his aid from an island on which he has been washed. Soon, he comes near enough to reach Frank with a pole, which he extends toward him. The latter lets go the rock, grasps the pole, and is pulled ashore. Seneca Howland is washed farther down the island, and is caught by some rocks, and, though somewhat bruised, manages to get ashore in safety. This seems a long time, as I tell it, but it is quickly done.

And now the three men are on an island, with a swift, dangerous river on either side, and a fall below. The *Emma Dean* is soon brought down, and Sumner, starting above as far as possible, pushes out. Right skillfully he plies the oars, and a few strokes set him on the island at the proper point. Then they all pull the boat up stream, as far as they are able, until they stand in water up to their necks. One sits on a rock, and holds the boat until the others are ready to pull, then gives the boat a push, clings to it with his hands, and climbs in as they pull for mainland, which they reach in safety. We are as glad to shake hands with them as though they had been on a voyage around the world, and wrecked on a distant coast.

Down the river half a mile we find that the after cabin of the wrecked boat, with a part of the bottom, ragged and splintered, has floated against a rock, and stranded. There are valuable articles in the cabin; but, on examination, we determine that life should not be risked to save them. Of course, the cargo of rations, instruments, and clothing is gone.

We return to the boats, and make camp for the night. No sleep comes to me in all those dark hours. The rations, instruments, and clothing have been divided among the boats, anticipating such an accident as this; and we started with duplicates of everything that was deemed necessary to success. But, in the distribution, there was one exception to this precaution, and the barometers were all placed in one boat, and they are lost. There is a possibility that they are in the cabin lodged against the rock, for that is where they were kept. But, then, how to reach them! The river is rising. Will they be there tomorrow? Can I go out to Salt Lake City, and obtain barometers from New York?

June 10.

I have determined to get the barometers from the wreck, if they are there. After breakfast, while the men make the portage, I go down

Fluted limestone in Marble Canyon, just below 25-Mile Canyon.

again for another examination. There the cabin lies, only carried fifty or sixty feet farther on.

Carefully looking over the ground, I am satisfied that it can be reached with safety, and return to tell the men my conclusion. Sumner and Dunn volunteer to take the little boat and make the attempt. They start, reach it, and out come the barometers; and now the boys set up a shout, and I join them, pleased that they should be as glad to save the instruments as myself. When the boat lands on our side, I find that the only things saved from the wreck were the barometers, a package of thermometers, and a three-gallon keg of whisky, which is what the men were shouting about. They had taken it aboard, unknown to me, and now I am glad they did, for they think it will do them good, as they are drenched every day by the melting snow, which runs down from the summits of the Rocky Mountains.

Now we come back to our work at the portage. We find that it is necessary to carry our rations over the rocks for nearly a mile, and let our boats down with lines, except at a few points, where they also must be carried. . . .

While the men are building the campfire, we discover an iron bake oven, several tin plates, a part of a boat, and many other fragments, which denote that this is the place where Ashley's party was wrecked.

June 11.

This day is spent in carrying our rations down to the bay—no small task to climb over the rocks with sacks of flour or bacon. We carry them by stages of about 500 yards each, and when night comes, and the last sack is on the beach, we are tired, bruised, and glad to sleep.

Wreck at Disaster Falls.

June 12.

Today we take the boats down to the bay. While at this work, we discover three sacks of flour from the wrecked boat, that have lodged in the rocks. We carry them above high water mark, and leave them, as our cargoes are already too heavy for the three remaining boats. We also find two or three oars, which we place with them.

As Ashley and his party were wrecked here, and as we have lost one of our boats at the same place, we adopt the name Disaster Falls for the scene of so much peril and loss.

Though some of his companions were drowned, Ashley and one other survived the wreck, climbed the canyon wall, and found their way across the Wasatch Mountains to Salt Lake City, living chiefly on berries, as they wandered through an unknown and difficult country. When they arrived at Salt Lake, they were almost destitute of clothing, and nearly starved. The Mormon people gave them food and clothing, and employed them to work on the foundation of the Temple, until they had earned sufficient to enable them to leave the country. Of their subsequent history, I have no knowledge. It is possible they returned to the scene of the disaster, as a little creek entering the river below is known as Ashley's Creek, and it is reported that he built a cabin and trapped on this river for one or two winters; but this may have been before the disaster.

June 13-15.

Rocks, rapids, and portages. . . . Here we have three falls in close succession. At the first, the water is compressed into a very narrow channel, against the right-hand cliff, and falls fifteen feet in ten yards; at the second, we have a broad sheet of water, tumbling down twenty feet over a group of rocks that thrust their dark heads through the foaming waters. The third is a broken fall, or short, abrupt rapid, where the water makes a descent of more than twenty feet among huge, fallen fragments of the cliff. We name the group Triplet Falls.

We make a portage around the first; past the second and third we let down with lines.

During the afternoon, Dunn and Howland, having returned from their climb, we run down, three-quarters of a mile, on quiet water, and land at the head of another fall. On examination, we find that there is an abrupt plunge of a few feet, and then the river tumbles, for half a mile, with a descent of a hundred feet, in a channel beset with great numbers of huge boulders. This stretch of the river is named Hell's Half-Mile.

The remaining portion of the day is occupied in making a trail among the rocks to the foot of the rapid.

June 16.

Our first work this morning is to carry our cargoes to the foot of the falls. Then we commence letting down the boats. We take two of them down in safety, but not without great difficulty; for, where such a vast body of water, rolling down an inclined plane, is broken into eddies and cross currents by rocks projecting from the cliffs and piles

The Green River at the Canyon of Lodore.

of boulders in the channel, it requires excessive labor and much care to prevent their being dashed against the rocks or breaking away. Sometimes we are compelled to hold the boat against a rock, above a chute, until a second line, attached to the stem, is carried to some point below, and, when all is ready, the first line is detached, and the boat given to the current, when she shoots down, and the men below swing her into some eddy.

At such a place, we are letting down the last boat, and, as she is set free, a wave turns her broadside down the stream, with the stem, to which the line is attached, from shore, and a little up. They haul on the line to bring the boat in, but the power of the current, striking obliquely against her, shoots her out into the middle of the river. The men have their hands burned with the friction of the passing line; the boat breaks away, and speeds, with great velocity, down the stream.

The *Maid of the Canyon* is lost, so it seems; but she drifts some distance, and swings into an eddy, in which she spins about, until we arrive with the small boat, and rescue her.

Soon we are on our way again, and stop at the mouth of a little brook, on the right, for a late dinner. . . .

Late in the afternoon we make a short run to the mouth of another little creek, coming down from the left into an alcove filled with luxuriant vegetation. Here camp is made with a group of cedars on one side and a dense mass of box-elders and dead willows on the other.

I go up to explore the alcove. While away a whirlwind comes, scattering the fire among the dead willows and cedar-spray, and soon there is a conflagration. The men rush for the boats, leaving all they cannot readily seize at the moment, and even then they have their clothing burned and hair singed, and Bradley has his ears scorched. The cook fills his arms with the mess kit,* and, jumping into a boat, stumbles and falls, and away go our cooking utensils into the river. Our plates are gone; our spoons are gone; our knives and forks are gone. "Water catch 'em; h-e-a-p catch 'em."

When on the boats, the men are compelled to cut loose, as the flames, running out on the overhanging willows, are scorching them. Loose on the stream, they must go down, for the water is too swift to make headway against it. Just below is a rapid, filled with rocks. On they

Limestone boulder near Vasey's Paradise, Marble Canyon. In 1969 "Marble" became a national monument.

* The mess kit was recovered on the second trip.

shoot, no channel explored, no signal to guide them. Just at this juncture I chance to see them, but have not yet discovered the fire, and the strange movements of the men fill me with astonishment. Down the rocks I clamber, and run to the bank. When I arrive, they have landed. Then we all go back to the late camp to see if anything left behind can be saved. Some of the clothing and bedding taken out of the boats is found, also a few tin cups, basins, and a camp kettle, and this is all the mess kit we now have. Yet we do just as well as ever.

June 17.
We run down to the mouth of Yampa River. This has been a chapter of disasters and toils, notwithstanding which the Canyon of Lodore was not devoid of scenic interest, even beyond the power of pen to tell. The roar of its waters was heard unceasingly from the hour we entered it until we landed here. No quiet in all that time. But its walls and cliffs, its peaks and crags, its amphitheaters and alcoves, tell a story of beauty and grandeur that I hear yet—and shall hear.

# From Echo Park to the Mouth of the Uinta River

The Yampa enters the Green from the east. At a point opposite its mouth, the Green runs to the south, at the foot of a rock, about seven hundred feet high and a mile long, and then turns sharply around it to the right, and runs back in a northerly course, parallel to its former direction, for nearly another mile, thus having the opposite sides of a long, narrow rock for its bank. The tongue of rock so formed is a peninsular precipice, with a mural escarpment along its whole course on the east, but broken down at places on the west. . . .

Great hollow domes are seen in the eastern side of the rock, against which the Green sweeps; willows border the river; clumps of box-elder are seen; and a few cottonwoods stand at the lower end. Standing opposite the rock, our words are repeated with startling clearness, but in a soft, mellow tone, that transforms them into magical music.

Scarcely can you believe it is the echo of your own voice. In some places two or three echoes come back; in other places they repeat themselves, passing back and forth across the river between this rock and the eastern wall.

To hear these repeated echoes well you must shout. Some of the party aver that ten or twelve repetitions can be heard. To me, they seem to rapidly diminish and merge by multiplicity, like telegraph poles on an outstretched plain. I have observed the same phenomenon once before in the cliffs near Long's Peak, and am pleased to meet with it again. . . .

June 18.

We have named the long peninsular rock on the other side Echo Rock. Desiring to climb it, Bradley and I take the little boat and pull up stream as far as possible, for it cannot be climbed directly opposite. We land on a talus of rocks at the upper end, to reach a place where it seems practicable to make the ascent; but we must go still farther up the river. So we scramble along, until we reach a place where the river sweeps against the wall. Here we find a shelf, along which we can pass, and now are ready for the climb.

We start up a gulch; then pass to the left, on a bench, along the wall; then up again, over broken rocks; then we reach more benches, along which we walk, until we find more broken rocks and crevices, by which we climb, still up, until we have ascended six or eight hundred feet; then we are met by a sheer precipice.

Looking about, we find a place where it seems possible to climb. I go ahead; Bradley hands the barometer to me, and follows. So we proceed, stage by stage, until we are nearly to the summit. Here, by making a spring, I gain a foothold in a little crevice, and grasp an angle of the rock overhead. I find I can get up no farther, and cannot step back, for I dare not let go with my hand, and cannot reach foothold below without. I call to Bradley for help. He finds a way by which he can get to the top of the rock over my head, but cannot reach me. Then he looks around for some stick or limb of a tree, but finds none. Then he suggests that he had better help me with the barometer case; but I fear I cannot hold on to it. The moment is critical. Standing on my toes, my muscles begin to tremble. It is sixty or eighty feet to the foot of the precipice. If I lose my hold I shall fall to the bottom, and then perhaps roll over the bench, and

Rescue of the one-armed leader.

tumble still farther down the cliff. At this instant it occurs to Bradley to take off his drawers, which he does, and swings them down to me. I hug close to the rock, let go with my hand, seize the dangling legs, and, with his assistance, I am enabled to gain the top.*

Then we walk out on a peninsular rock, make the necessary observations for determining its altitude above camp, and return, finding an easy way down.

June 19.

Today, Howland, Bradley, and I take the *Emma Dean,* and start up the Yampa River.† The stream is much swollen, the current swift, and we are able to make but slow progress against it. The canyon in this part of the course of the Yampa is cut through light-gray sandstone. The river is very winding, and the swifter water is usually found on the outside of the curve, sweeping against vertical cliffs, often a thousand feet high. In the center of these curves, in many places, the rock above overhangs the river. On the opposite side, the walls are broken, craggy, and sloping, and occasionally side canyons enter. When we have rowed until we are quite tired we stop, and take advantage of one of these broken places to climb out of the canyon. When above, we can look up the Yampa for a distance of several miles.

June 20.

This morning two of the men take me up the Yampa for a short distance, and I go out to climb. Having reached the top of the canyon, I walk over long stretches of naked sandstone, crossing gulches now and then, and by noon reach the summit of Mount Dawes. From this point I can look away to the north, and see in the dim distance the Sweetwater and Wind River Mountains, more than a hundred miles away. To the northwest, the Wasatch Mountains are in view and peaks of the Uinta. To the east, I can see the western slopes of the Rocky Mountains, more than a hundred and fifty miles distant. . . .

June 21.

We float around the long rock, and enter another canyon. The walls are high and vertical; the canyon is narrow; and the river fills the whole space below, so that there is no landing-place at the foot of the

---

* Bradley indicates this happened on July 8, 1869, many miles downstream from this point.
† No trip was made up the Yampa in 1869. Trip was made in *Emma Dean* No. 2 with S. V. Jones, J. K. Hillers, E. O. Beaman, and Andy Hattan—June 27-30, 1871.

Small rapid in Marble Gorge.

cliff. The Green is greatly increased by the Yampa, and we now have a much larger river. All this volume of water, confined, as it is, in a narrow channel, and rushing with great velocity, is set eddying and spinning in whirlpools by projecting rocks and short curves, and the waters waltz their way through the canyon, making their own rippling, rushing, roaring music. The canyon is much narrower than any we have seen. With difficulty we manage our boats. They spin about from side to side, and we know not where we are going, and find it impossible to keep them headed down the stream. At first, this causes us great alarm, but we soon find there is but little danger, and that there is a general movement of progression down the river, to which this whirling is but an adjunct; and it is the merry mood of the river to dance through this deep, dark gorge; and right gaily do we join in the sport.

Soon our revel is interrupted by a cataract; its roaring command is heeded by all our power at the oars, and we pull against the whirling current. The *Emma Dean* is brought up against a cliff, about fifty feet above the brink of the fall. By vigorously plying the oars on the side opposite the wall, as if to pull up stream, we can hold her against the rock. The boats behind are signaled to land where they can. The *Maid of the Canyon* is pulled to the left wall, and, by constant rowing, they can hold her also. The *Sister* is run into an alcove on the right, where an eddy is in a dance, and in this she joins. Now my little boat is held against the wall only by the utmost exertion, and it is impossible to make headway against the current. On examination, I find a horizontal crevice in the rock, about ten feet above the water, and a boat's length below us, so we let her down to that point. One of the men clambers into the crevice, in which he can just crawl; we toss him the line, which he makes fast in the rocks, and now our boat is tied up. Then I follow into the crevice, and we crawl along a distance of fifty feet, or more, up stream, and find a broken place, where we can climb about fifty feet higher. Here we stand on a shelf, that passes along down stream to a point above the falls, where it is broken down, and a pile of rocks, over which we can descend to the river, is lying against the foot of the cliff.

It has been mentioned that one of the boats is on the other side. I signal for the men to pull her up alongside of the wall, but it cannot be done; then to cross. This they do, gaining the wall on our side just above where the *Emma Dean* is tied.

The third boat is out of sight, whirling in the eddy of a recess. Looking about, I find another horizontal crevice, along which I crawl to a point just over the water, where this boat is lying, and, calling loud and long, I finally succeed in making the crew understand that I want them to bring the boat down, hugging the wall. This they accomplish, by taking advantage of every crevice and knob on the face of the cliff, so that we have the three boats together at a point a few yards above the falls. Now, by passing a line up on the shelf, the boats can be let down to the broken rocks below. This we do, and, making a short portage, our troubles here are over.

Below the falls, the canyon is wider, and there is more or less space between the river and the walls; but the stream, though wide, is rapid, and rolls at a fearful rate among the rocks. We proceed with great caution, and run the large boats altogether by signal. . . .

A side canyon, 1872.

June 22.

After dinner, we start; the large boats are to follow in fifteen minutes, and look out for the signal to land. Into the middle of the stream we row, and down the rapid river we glide, only making strokes enough with the oars to guide the boat. What a headlong ride it is! shooting past rocks and islands! I am soon filled with exhilaration only experienced before in riding a fleet horse over the outstretched prairie. One, two, three, four miles we go, rearing and plunging with the waves, until we wheel to the right into a beautiful park, and land on an island, where we go into camp. . . .

June 23.

We remain in camp today to repair our boats, which have had hard knocks, and are leaking. Two of the men go out with the barometer to climb the cliff at the foot of Whirlpool Canyon and measure the walls; another goes on the mountain to hunt; and Bradley and I spend the day among the rocks, studying an interesting geologic fold and collecting fossils. Late in the afternoon the hunter returns and brings with him a fine, fat deer; so we give his name to the mountain— Mount Hawkins. Just before night we move camp to the lower end of the park, floating down the river about four miles.

June 24.

Bradley and I start early to climb the mountain ridge to the east, and find its summit to be nearly three thousand feet above camp. It has required some labor to scale it; but on its top, what a view!* There is a long spur running out from the Uinta Mountains toward the south, and the river runs lengthwise through it.

We are standing three thousand feet above the waters, which are troubled with billows and are white with foam. The walls are set with crags and peaks and buttressed towers and overhanging domes. Turning to the right, the park is below us, its island groves reflected by the deep, quiet waters. Rich meadows stretch out on either hand to the verge of a sloping plain that comes down from the distant mountains. These plains are of almost naked rock, in strange contrast to the meadows—blue and lilac-colored rocks, buff and pink, vermilion and brown, and all these colors clear and bright. A dozen little creeks, dry the greater part of the year, run down through the half circle of exposed formations, radiating from the island-center to the rim of the basin. Each creek has its system of side streams, and each side stream has its system of laterals, and, again, these are divided, so that this outstretched slope of rock is elaborately embossed. Beds of different colored formations run in parallel bands on either side. The perspective, modified by the undulations, gives the bands a waved appearance, and the high colors gleam in the midday sun with the luster of satin. We are tempted to call this Rainbow Park. Away beyond these beds are the Uinta and Wasatch Mountains, with their pine forests and snow fields and naked peaks. Now we turn to the right, and look up Whirlpool Canyon, a deep gorge, with a river in the bottom—a gloomy chasm, where mad waves roar; but, at this distance and altitude, the river is but a rippling brook, and the chasm a narrow cleft. The top of the mountain on which we stand is a broad, grassy table, and a herd of deer is feeding in the distance. Walking over to the southeast, we look down into the valley of White River, and beyond that see the far distant Rocky Mountains, in mellow, perspective haze, through which snow fields shine.

June 25.

This morning, we enter Split Mountain Canyon, sailing in through a broad, flaring, brilliant gateway. We run two or three rapids after they have been carefully examined. Then we have a series of six or eight, over which we are compelled to pass by letting the boats down

Sand bar at Redwall Cavern.

* Bradley's diary says that Powell climbed a mountain and Bradley went to recover a quarter of a deer, not on the same mountain.

58

with lines. This occupies the entire day, and we camp at night at the mouth of a great cave. . . .

June 26.

At three o'clock we are all aboard again. Down the river we are carried by the swift waters at great speed, sheering around a rock now and then with a timely stroke or two of the oars. At one point, the river turns from left to right, in a direction at right angles to the canyon, in a long chute, and strikes the right, where its waters are heaped up in great billows, that tumble back in breakers. We glide into the chute before we see the danger, and it is too late to stop. Two or three hard strokes are given on the right, and we pause for an instant, expecting to be dashed against the rock. The bow of the boat leaps high on a great wave; the rebounding waters hurl us back, and the peril is past. The next moment, the other boats are hurriedly signaled to land on the left. Accomplishing this, the men walk along the shore, holding the boats near the bank, and let them drift around. Starting again, we soon debouch into a beautiful valley, and glide down its length for ten miles, and camp under a grand old cottonwood. This is evidently a frequent resort for Indians. Tent poles are lying about, and the dead embers of late campfires are seen. On the plains, to the left, antelope are feeding. Now and then a wolf is seen, and after dark they make the air resound with their howling.

One of the 1871–72 boats being repaired.

June 27-30.

Now our way is along a gently flowing river, beset with many islands; groves are seen on either side, and natural meadows, where herds of antelope are feeding. Here and there we have views of the distant mountains on the right. . . .

Up the valley of this stream, about forty miles, the reservation of the Uinta Indians is situated. We propose to go there, and see if we can replenish our mess kit, and, perhaps, send letters to friends. We also desire to establish an astronomic station here; and hence this will be our stopping place for several days. . . .

July 1.

Two days have been employed in obtaining the local time, taking observations for latitude and longitude, and making excursions into the adjacent country. This morning, with two of the men, I start for

Buck Farm Canyon, mile 40, in Marble Canyon.

the Uinta Agency. It is a toilsome walk, twenty miles of the distance being across a sand desert. Occasionally, we have to wade the river, crossing it back and forth. Toward evening, we cross several beautiful streams, which are tributaries of the Uinta, and we pass through pine groves and meadows, arriving just at dusk at the Reservation. Captain Dodds, the agent, is away, having gone to Salt Lake City, but his assistants receive us very kindly. It is rather pleasant to see a house once more, and some evidences of civilization, even if it is on an Indian reservation, several days' ride from the nearest home of the white man.

Warrior and bride (Ute Indians).

July 2.

I go, this morning, to visit *Tsau'-wi-at*. This old chief is but the wreck of a man, and no longer has influence. Looking at him, you can scarcely realize that he is a man. His skin is shrunken, wrinkled, and dry, and seems to cover no more than a form of bones. He is said to be more than a hundred years old. I talk a little with him, but his conversation is incoherent, though he seems to take pride in showing me some medals, that must have been given him many years ago. He has a pipe which, he says, he has used a long time. I offer to exchange with him, and he seems to be glad to accept; so I add another to my collection of pipes. His wife, "The Bishop," as she is called, is a very garrulous old woman; she exerts a great influence, and is much revered. She is the only Indian woman I have known to occupy a place in the council ring. She seems very much younger than her husband, and, though wrinkled and ugly, is still vigorous. She has much to say to me concerning the condition of the people, and seems very anxious that they should learn to cultivate the soil, own farms, and live like white men. After talking a couple of hours with these old people, I go to see the farms. They are situated in a very beautiful district, where many fine streams of water meander across alluvial plains and meadows. These creeks have quite a fall, and it is very easy to take their waters out above, and, with them, overflow the lands.

It will be remembered that irrigation is necessary, in this dry climate, to successful farming. Quite a number of Indians have each a patch of ground, of two or three acres, on which they are raising wheat, potatoes, turnips, pumpkins, melons, and other vegetables. Most of the crops are looking well, and it is rather surprising with what pride they show us that they are able to cultivate crops like white men. They are still occupying lodges, and refuse to build houses, assigning as a reason that when anyone dies in a lodge it is always abandoned, and very often burned with all the effects of the deceased, and when houses have been built for them they have been treated in the same way. With their unclean habits, a fixed residence would doubtless be no pleasant place. This beautiful valley has been the home of a people of a higher grade of civilization than the present Utes. Evidences of this are quite abundant; on our way here yesterday we discovered, in many places along the trail, fragments of pottery; and wandering about the little farms today, I find the foundations of ancient houses, and mealing stones that were not used by nomadic people, as they are too heavy to be transported by such tribes, and are deeply worn. The Indians, seeing that I am interested in these matters, take pains to show me several other places where these evidences remain, and tell me that they know nothing about the people who formerly dwelt here. They further tell me that up the canyon the rocks are covered with pictures. . . .

Juniper shelters of the Unkakaniguts.

July 5.

Frank Goodman informs me, this morning, that he has concluded not to go on with the party, saying that he has seen danger enough. It will be remembered that he was one of the crew on the *No Name,* when she was wrecked. As our boats are rather heavily loaded, I am content that he should leave, although he has been a faithful man. . . .

# From the Mouth of the Uinta River to the Junction of the Grand and Green

July 6.

Start early this morning. A short distance below the mouth of the Uinta, we come to the head of a long island. Last winter, a man named Johnson, a hunter and Indian trader, visited us at our camp in White River Valley. This man has an Indian wife, and, having no fixed home, usually travels with one of the Ute bands. He informed me it

[following page]
Side canyon near the abandoned Marble Gorge dam site.

was his intention to plant some corn, potatoes, and other vegetables on this island in the spring, and, knowing that we would pass it, invited us to stop and help ourselves, even if he should not be there; so we land and go out on the island. Looking about, we soon discover his garden, but it is in a sad condition, having received no care since it was planted. It is yet too early in the season for corn, but Hall suggests that potato tops are good greens, and, anxious for some change from our salt meat fare, we gather a quantity and take them aboard. At noon we stop and cook our greens for dinner; but soon, one after another of the party is taken sick; nausea first, and then severe vomiting, and we tumble around under the trees, groaning with pain, and I feel a little alarmed, lest our poisoning be severe. Emetics are administered to those who are willing to take them, and about the middle of the afternoon we are all rid of the pain. Jack Sumner records in his diary that "Potato tops are not good greens on the sixth day of July."

This evening we enter another canyon, almost imperceptibly, as the walls rise very gently.

July 7.
We find quiet water today, the river sweeping in great and beautiful curves, the canyon walls steadily increasing in altitude. The escarpment formed by the cut edges of the rock are often vertical, sometimes terraced, and in some places the treads of the terraces are sloping. In these quiet curves vast amphitheaters are formed, now in vertical rocks, now in steps. . . .

July 8.
After dinner, we pass through a region of the wildest desolation. The canyon is very tortuous, the river very rapid, and many lateral canyons enter on either side. These usually have their branches, so that the region is cut into a wilderness of gray and brown cliffs. In several places, these lateral canyons are only separated from each other by narrow walls, often hundreds of feet high, but so narrow in places that where softer rocks are found below, they have crumbled away, and left holes in the wall, forming passages from one canyon into another. These we often call natural bridges; but they were never intended to span streams. They had better, perhaps, be called side doors between canyon chambers.

The walls are almost without vegetation; a few dwarf bushes are seen here and there, clinging to the rocks, and cedars grow from the crevices—not like the cedars of a land refreshed with rains, great cones bedecked with spray, but ugly clumps, like war clubs, beset with spines. We are minded to call this the Canyon of Desolation.

The wind annoys us much today. The water, rough by reason of the rapids, is made more so by head gales. Wherever a great face of rock has a southern exposure, the rarified air rises, and the wind rushes in below, either up or down the canyon, or both, causing local currents.

Just at sunset, we run a bad rapid, and camp at its foot.

Canyon of Desolation.

July 9.
During the afternoon, we come to a rather open canyon valley, stretching up toward the west, its farther end lost in the mountains. From a point to which we climb, we obtain a good view of its course, until its angular walls are lost in the vista.

July 10.
Sumner, who is a fine mechanist, is learning to take observations for time with the sextant. Today, he remains in camp to practice.

Howland Dunn and myself determine to climb out, and start up a lateral canyon, taking a barometer with us, for the purpose of measuring the thickness of the strata over which we pass. The readings of a barometer below are recorded every half hour, and our observations must be simultaneous. Where the beds, which we desire to measure, are very thick, we must climb with the utmost speed, to reach their summits in time. Again, where there are thinner beds, we wait for the moment to arrive; and so, by hard and easy stages, we make our way to the top of the canyon wall, and reach the plateau above about two o'clock. . . .

The elevation of the plateau being about eight thousand feet above the level of the sea, brings it into a region of moisture, as is well attested by the forests and grassy valleys. The plateau seems to rise gradually to the west, until it merges into the Wasatch Mountains. On these high table lands, elk and deer abound; and they are favorite hunting grounds for the Ute Indians.

A little before sunset, Howland and I meet again at the head of the side canyon, and down we start. It is late, and we must make great

haste, or be caught by the darkness; so we go, running where we can; leaping over the ledges; letting each other down on the loose rocks, as long as we can see. When darkness comes, we are still some distance from camp, and a long, slow, anxious descent we make, toward the gleaming campfire.

After supper, observations for latitude are taken, and only two or three hours for sleep remain, before daylight.

July 11.

A short distance below camp we run a rapid, and, in doing so, break an oar, and then lose another, both belonging to the *Emma Dean*. So the pioneer boat has but two oars.

We see nothing of which oars can be made, so we conclude to run on to some point, where it seems possible to climb out to the forests on the plateau, and there we will procure suitable timber from which to make new ones.

We soon approach another rapid. Standing on deck, I think it can be run, and on we go. Coming nearer, I see that at the foot it has a short turn to the left, where the waters pile up against the cliff. Here we try to land, but quickly discover that, being in swift water, above the fall, we cannot reach shore, crippled, as we are, by the loss of two oars; so the bow of the boat is turned down stream. We shoot by a big rock; a reflex wave rolls over our little boat and fills her. I see the place is dangerous, and quickly signal to the other boats to land where they can. This is scarcely completed when another wave rolls our boat over, and I am thrown some distance into the water. I soon find that swimming is very easy, and I cannot sink. It is only necessary to ply strokes sufficient to keep my head out of the water, though now and then, when a breaker rolls over me, I close my mouth, and am carried through it. The boat is drifting ahead of me twenty or thirty feet, and, when the great waves are passed, I overtake it, and find Sumner and Dunn clinging to her. As soon as we reach quiet water, we all swim to one side and turn her over. In doing this, Dunn loses his hold and goes under; when he comes up, he is caught by Sumner and pulled to the boat. In the meantime we have drifted down stream some distance, and see another rapid below. How bad it may be we cannot tell, so we swim toward shore, pulling our boat with us, with all the vigor possible, but are carried down much faster than distance toward shore is gained. At last we reach a huge pile of driftwood. Our rolls of

Entrance to Lava Canyon in the Grand Canyon. This is the start of what Powell called "the trip down the Great Unknown."

blankets, two guns, and a barometer were in the open compartment of the boat, and, when it went over, these were thrown out. The guns and barometer are lost, but I succeeded in catching one of the rolls of blankets, as it drifted by, when we were swimming to shore; the other two are lost, and sometimes hereafter we may sleep cold.

A huge fire is built on the bank, our clothing is spread to dry, and then from the drift logs we select one from which we think oars can be made, and the remainder of the day is spent in sawing them out.

July 12.

This morning, the new oars are finished, and we start once more. We pass several bad rapids, making a short portage at one, and before noon we come to a long, bad fall, where the channel is filled with rocks on the left, turning the waters to the right, where they pass under an overhanging rock. On examination, we determine to run it, keeping as close to the left-hand rocks as safety will permit, in order to avoid the overhanging cliff. The little boat runs over all right; another follows, but the men are not able to keep her near enough to the left bank, and she is carried, by a swift chute, into great waves to the right, where she is tossed about, and Bradley is knocked over the side, but his foot catching under the seat, he is dragged along in the water, with his head down; making great exertion, he seizes the gunwale with his left hand, and can lift his head above water now and then. To us who are below, it seems impossible to keep the boat from going under the overhanging cliff; but Powell, for the moment, heedless of Bradley's mishap, pulls with all his power for half a dozen strokes, when the danger is past; then he seizes Bradley, and pulls him in. The men in the boat above, seeing this, land, and she is let down by lines.

Just here we emerge from the Canyon of Desolation, as we have named it, into a more open country, which extends for a distance of nearly a mile, when we enter another canyon, cut through gray sandstone.

About three o'clock in the afternoon we meet with a new difficulty. The river fills the entire channel; the walls are vertical on either side, from the water's edge, and a bad rapid is beset with rocks. We come to the head of it, and land on a rock in the stream; the little boat is let down to another rock below, the men of the larger boat holding to the line; the second boat is let down in the same way, and the line of the third boat is brought with them. Now, the third boat pushes out from the upper rock, and, as we have her line below, we pull in and catch her, as she is sweeping by at the foot of the rock on which we stand. Again the first boat is let down stream the full length of her line, and the second boat is passed down by the first to the extent of her line, which is held by the men in the first boat; so she is two lines' length from where she started. Then the third boat is let down past the second, and still down, nearly to the length of her line, so that she is fast to the second boat, and swinging down three lines' lengths, with the other two boats intervening. Held in this way, the men are able to pull her into a cove, in the left wall, where she is made fast. But this leaves a man on the rock above, holding to the line of the little boat. When all is ready, he springs from the rock, clinging to the line with one hand, and swimming with the other, and we pull him in as he goes by. As the two boats, thus loosened, drift down, the men in the cove pull us all in, as we come opposite; then we pass around to a point of rock below the cove, close to the wall, land, and make a short portage over the worst places in the rapid, and start again.

At night we camp on a sand beach; the wind blows a hurricane; the drifting sand almost blinds us; and nowhere can we find shelter. The wind continues to blow all night; the sand sifts through our blankets, and piles over us, until we are covered as in a snowdrift. We are glad when morning comes.

Gunnison Butte, Gray Canyon.

July 13.

This morning, we have an exhilarating ride. The river is swift, and there are many smooth rapids. I stand on deck, keeping careful watch ahead, and we glide along, mile after mile, plying strokes now on the right, and then on the left, just sufficient to guide our boats past the rocks into smooth water. At noon we emerge from Gray Canyon, as we have named it, and camp, for dinner, under a cottonwood tree, standing on the left bank.

Extensive sand plains extend back from the immediate river valley, as far as we can see, on either side. These naked, drifting sands gleam brilliantly in the midday sun of July. The reflected heat from the glaring surface produces a curious motion of the atmosphere; little currents are generated, and the whole seems to be trembling and moving about in many directions, or, failing to see that the movement is in the atmosphere, it gives the impression of an unstable land. Plains, and hills, and cliffs, and distant mountains seem vaguely to be floating about in a trembling, wave-rocked sea, and patches of landscape will seem to float away, and be lost, and then re-appear. . . .

About two hours from noon camp, we discover an Indian crossing, where a number of rafts, rudely constructed of logs and bound together by withes, are floating against the bank. On landing, we see evidences that a party of Indians have crossed within a very few days. This is the place where the lamented Gunnison crossed, in the year 1853, when making an exploration for a railroad route to the Pacific coast. . . .

July 14.
This morning, we pass some curious black bluffs on the right, then two or three short canyons, and then we discover the mouth of the San Rafael, a stream which comes down from the distant mountains in the west.

Now, we enter another canyon. Gradually the walls rise higher and higher as we proceed, and the summit of the canyon is formed of the same beds of orange-colored sandstone. Back from the brink, the hollows of the plateau are filled with sands disintegrated from these orange beds. They are of rich cream color, shaded into maroon, everywhere destitute of vegetation, and drifted into long, wave-like ridges.

The course of the river is tortuous, and it nearly doubles upon itself many times. The water is quiet, and constant rowing is necessary to make much headway. Sometimes, there is a narrow flood-plain between the river and the wall, on one side or the other. Where these long, gentle curves are found, the river washes the very foot of the outer wall. A long peninsula of willow-bordered meadow projects within the curve, and the talus, at the foot of the cliff, is usually covered with dwarf oaks. The orange-colored sandstone is very homogenous in structure, and the walls are usually vertical, though not very high. Where the river sweeps around a curve under a cliff, a vast hollow dome may be seen, with many caves and deep alcoves, that are greatly admired by the members of the party, as we go by.

We camp at night on the left bank. . . .

July 15.
There is an exquisite charm in our ride today down this beautiful canyon. It gradually grows deeper with every mile of travel; the walls are symmetrically curved, and grandly arched; of a beautiful color,

Schist sculptured by water and time in the narrow Inner Gorge.

and reflected in the quiet waters in many places, so as to almost deceive the eye, and suggest the thought, to the beholder, that he is looking into profound depths. We are all in fine spirits, feel very gay, and the badinage of the men is echoed from wall to wall. Now and then we whistle, or shout, or discharge a pistol, to listen to the reverberations among the cliffs.

At night we camp on the south side of the great Bow-knot, and, as we eat our supper, which is spread on the beach, we name this Labyrinth Canyon.

July 16.

Still we go down, on our winding way. We pass tower cliffs, then we find the river widens out for several miles, and meadows are seen on either side, between the river and the walls. We name this expansion of the river Tower Park. . . .

July 17.

We are now down among the buttes, and in a region, the surface of which is naked, solid rock—a beautiful red sandstone, forming a smooth, undulating pavement. The Indians call this the *"Toom'-pin Tu-weap',"* or "Rock Land," and sometimes the *"Toom'-pin wu-near' Tu-weap',"* or "Land of Standing Rock."

The Land of the Standing Rocks.

Off to the south we see a butte, in the form of a fallen cross. It is several miles away, still it presents no inconspicuous figure on the landscape, and must be many hundreds of feet high, probably more than two thousand. We note its position on our map, and name it "The Butte of the Cross."*

We continue our journey. In many places the walls, which rise from the water's edge, are overhanging on either side. The stream is still quiet, and we glide along, through a strange, weird, grand region. The landscape everywhere, away from the river, is of rock—cliffs of rock; tables of rock; plateaus of rock; terraces of rock; crags of rock—ten thousand strangely carved forms. Rocks everywhere, and no vegetation; no soil; no sand. In long, gentle curves, the river winds about these rocks.

When speaking of these rocks, we must not conceive of piles of boulders, or heaps of fragments, but a whole land of naked rock, with giant forms carved on it: cathedral-shaped buttes, towering hundreds or thousands of feet; cliffs that cannot be scaled, and canyon walls that shrink the river into insignificance, with vast, hollow domes, and tall pinnacles, and shafts set on the verge overhead, and all highly colored—buff, gray, red, brown, and chocolate; never lichened; never moss-covered; but bare, and often polished. . . .

Late in the afternoon, the water becomes swift, and our boats make great speed. An hour of this rapid running brings us to the junction of the Grand and Green, the foot of Stillwater Canyon, as we have named it.†

These streams unite in solemn depths, more than one thousand two hundred feet below the general surface of the country. The walls of the lower end of Stillwater Canyon are very beautifully curved, as the river sweeps in its meandering course. The lower end of the canyon through which the Grand comes down is also regular, but much more direct, and we look up this stream, and out into the country beyond, and obtain glimpses of snow-clad peaks, the summits of a group of mountains known as the Sierra La Sal. Down the Colorado, the canyon walls are much broken.

We row around into the Grand, and camp on its northwest bank; and here we propose to stay several days, for the purpose of determining the latitude and longitude, and the altitude of the walls. Much of the night is spent in making observations with the sextant. . . .

* Named on September 12, 1871, according to Powell's second diary.
† July 16 according to other diaries.

On top, near the junction of the Grand (now Colorado) and Green rivers.

# From the Junction
of the Grand and Green
to the Mouth
of the Little Colorado

July 18.

The day is spent in obtaining the time, and spreading our rations, which, we find, are badly injured. The flour has been wet and dried so many times that it is all musty, and full of hard lumps. We make a sieve of mosquito netting, and run our flour through it, losing more than two hundred pounds by the process. Our losses, by the wrecking of the *No Name,* and by various mishaps since, together with the amount thrown away today, leave us little more than two months' supplies, and, to make them last thus long, we must be fortunate enough to lose no more.

We drag our boats on shore, and turn them over to recalk and pitch them, and Sumner is engaged in repairing barometers. While we are here, for a day or two, resting, we propose to put everything in the best shape for a vigorous campaign.

July 19.

Bradley and I start this morning to climb the left wall below the junction. The way we have selected is up a gulch. Climbing for an hour over and among the rocks, we find ourselves in a vast amphitheater, and our way cut off. We clamber around to the left for half an hour, until we find that we cannot go up in that direction. Then we try the rocks around to the right, and discover a narrow shelf, nearly half a mile long. In some places, this is so wide that we pass along with ease; in others, it is so narrow and sloping that we are compelled to lie down and crawl. We can look over the edge of the shelf, down eight hundred feet, and see the river rolling and plunging among the rocks. Looking up five hundred feet, to the brink of the cliff, it seems to blend with the sky. We continue along, until we come to a point where the wall is again broken down. Up we climb. On the right, there is a narrow, mural point of rocks, extending toward the river, two or three hundred feet high, and six or eight hundred feet long. We come back

Here Hillers poses before the heavy wet plate photographic equipment that was such a great chore to members of the second expedition. This equipment, including a dark box, was frequently dragged to heights of 2,000 or 3,000 feet.

Matcatameba Canyon in the Grand Canyon.

to where this sets in, and find it cut off from the main wall by a great crevice. Into this we pass. And now, a long, narrow rock is between us and the river. The rock itself is split longitudinally and transversely; and the rains on the surface above have run down through the crevices, and gathered into channels below, and then run off into the river. The crevices are usually narrow above, and, by erosion of the streams, wider below, forming a network of caves; but each cave having a narrow, winding skylight up through the rocks. We wander among these corridors for an hour or two, but find no place where the rocks are broken down, so that we can climb up. At last, we determine to attempt a passage by a crevice, and select one which we think is wide enough to admit of the passage of our bodies, and yet narrow enough to climb out by pressing our hands and feet against the walls. So we climb as men would out of a well. Bradley climbs first; I hand him the barometer, then climb over his head, and he hands me the barometer. So we pass each other alternately, until we emerge from the fissure, out on the summit of the rock. And what a world of grandeur is spread before us! Below is the canyon, through which the Colorado runs. We can trace its course for miles, and at points catch glimpses of the river. From the northwest comes the Green, in a narrow, winding gorge. From the northeast comes the Grand, through a canyon that seems bottomless from where we stand. Away to the west are lines of cliffs and ledges of rock—not such ledges as you may have seen where the quarryman splits his blocks, but ledges from which the gods might quarry mountains, that, rolled out on the plain below, would stand a lofty range; and not such cliffs as you may have seen where the swallow builds its nest, but cliffs where the soaring eagle is lost to view ere he reaches the summit. Between us and the distant cliffs are the strangely carved and pinnacled rocks of the *Toom'-pin wu-near' Tu-*

Upper view looking east,
with the Grand Canyon in the distance.

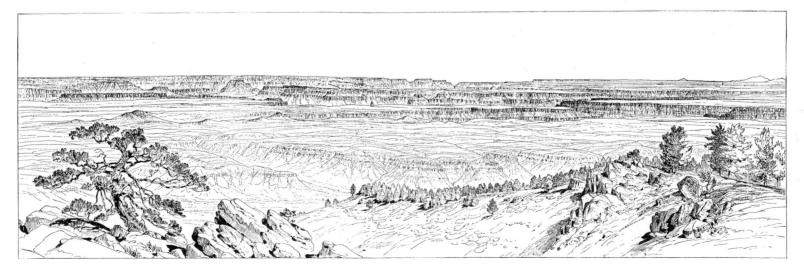

*weap'*. On the summit of the opposite wall of the canyon are rock forms that we do not understand. Away to the east a group of eruptive mountains are seen—the Sierra La Sal. Their slopes are covered with pines, and deep gulches are flanked with great crags, and snow fields are seen near the summits. So the mountains are in uniform, green, gray, and silver. Wherever we look there is but a wilderness of rocks; deep gorges, where the rivers are lost below cliffs and towers and pinnacles; and ten thousand strangely carved forms in every direction; and beyond them, mountains blending with the clouds.

Now we return to camp. While we are eating supper, we very naturally speak of better fare, as musty bread and spoiled bacon are not pleasant. Soon I see Hawkins down by the boat, taking up the sextant, rather a strange proceeding for him, and I question him concerning it. He replies that he is trying to find the latitude and longitude of the nearest pie.

July 20.

This morning, Captain Powell and I go out to climb the west wall of the canyon, for the purpose of examining the strange rocks seen yesterday from the other side.* Two hours bring us to the top, at a point between the Green and Colorado, overlooking the junction of the rivers. A long neck of rock extends toward the mouth of the Grand. Out on this we walk, crossing a great number of deep crevices. Usually, the smooth rock slopes down to the fissure on either side. Sometimes it is an interesting question to us whether the slope is not so steep that we cannot stand on it. Sometimes, starting down, we are compelled to go on, and we are not always sure that the crevice is not too wide for a jump, when we measure it with our eye from above. Probably the slopes would not be difficult if there was not a fissure at the lower end; nor would the fissures cause fear if they were but a few feet deep. It is curious how a little obstacle becomes a great obstruction, when a misstep would land a man in the bottom of a deep chasm. . . .

The course of the Green, at this point, is approximately at right angles to that of the Colorado, and on the brink of the latter canyon we find the same system of terraced and walled glens. The walls, and pinnacles, and towers are of sandstone, homogeneous in structure, but not in color, as they show broad bands of red, buff, and gray. This

* Probably a trek with Jones on September 12, 1871, or with Thompson on September 17.

painting of the rocks, dividing them into sections, increases their apparent height. In some places, these terraced and walled glens, along the Colorado, have coalesced with those along the Green; that is, the intervening walls are broken down. It is very rarely that a loose rock is seen. The sand is washed off so that the walls, terraces, and slopes of the glens are all of smooth sandstone.

In the walls themselves, curious caves and channels have been carved. In some places, there are little stairways up the walls; in others, the walls present what are known as royal arches; and so we wander through glens, and among pinnacles, and climb the walls from early morn until late in the afternoon.

Running a rapid.

## July 21.

We start this morning on the Colorado. The river is rough, and bad rapids, in close succession, are found. Two very hard portages are made during the forenoon. After dinner, in running a rapid, the *Emma Dean* is swamped, and we are thrown into the river, we cling to her, and in the first quiet water below she is righted and bailed out; but three oars are lost in this mishap. The larger boats land above the dangerous place, and we make a portage, that occupies all the afternoon. We camp at night, on the rocks on the left bank, and can scarcely find room to lie down.

## July 22.

This morning, we continue our journey, though short of oars. There is no timber growing on the walls within our reach, and no driftwood along the banks, so we are compelled to go on until something suitable can be found. A mile and three-quarters below, we find a huge pile of driftwood, among which are some cottonwood logs. From these we select one which we think the best, and the men are set at work sawing oars. Our boats are leaking again, from the strains received in the bad rapids yesterday, so, after dinner, they are turned over, and some of the men are engaged in calking them.

Captain Powell and I go out to climb the wall to the east, for we can see dwarf pines above, and it is our purpose to collect the resin which oozes from them, to use in pitching our boats. We take a barometer with us, and find that the walls are becoming higher, for now they register an altitude, above the river, of nearly fifteen hundred feet.

Ancient fluted schist.

July 23.

On starting, we come at once to difficult rapids and falls, that, in many places, are more abrupt than in any of the canyons through which we have passed, and we decide to name this Cataract Canyon.

From morning until noon, the course of the river is to the west; the scenery is grand, with rapids and falls below, and walls above, beset with crags and pinnacles. Just at noon we wheel again to the south, and go into camp for dinner.

While the cook is preparing it, Bradley, Captain Powell, and myself go up into a side canyon, that comes in at this point. We enter through a very narrow passage, having to wade along the course of a little stream until a cascade interrupts our progress. Then we climb to the right, for a hundred feet, until we reach a little shelf, along which we pass, walking with great care, for it is narrow, until we pass around the fall. Here the gorge widens into a spacious, sky-roofed chamber. In the farther end is a beautiful grove of cottonwoods, and between us and the cottonwoods the little stream widens out into three clear lakelets, with bottoms of smooth rock. Beyond the cottonwoods, the brook tumbles, in a series of white, shining cascades, from heights that seem immeasurable. Turning around, we can look through the cleft through which we came, and see the river, with towering walls beyond. What a chamber for a resting place is this! hewn from the solid rock; the heavens for a ceiling; cascade fountains within; a grove in the conservatory, clear lakelets for a refreshing bath, and an outlook through the doorway on a raging river, with cliffs and mountains beyond.

Our way, after dinner, is through a gorge, grand beyond description. The walls are nearly vertical; the river broad and swift, but free from rocks and falls. From the edge of the water to the brink of the cliffs it is one thousand six hundred to one thousand eight hundred feet. At this great depth, the river rolls in solemn majesty. . . .


July 24.

We examine the rapids below. Large rocks have fallen from the walls —great, angular blocks, which have rolled down the talus, and are strewn along the channel We are compelled to make three portages in succession, the distance being less than three-fourths of a mile, with a fall of seventy-five feet. Among these rocks, in chutes, whirlpools, and great waves, with rushing breakers and foam, the water finds its way, still tumbling down. We stop for the night, only three-fourths of a mile below the last camp. A very hard day's work has been done, and at evening I sit on a rock by the edge of the river, to look at the water, and listen to its roar. Hours ago, deep shadows had settled into the canyon as the sun passed behind the cliffs. Now, doubtless, the sun has gone down, for we can see no glint of light on the crags above. Darkness is coming on. The waves are rolling, with crests of foam so white they seem almost to give a light of their own. Near by, a chute of water strikes the foot of a great block of limestone, fifty feet high, and the waters pile up against it, and roll back. Where there are sunken rocks, the water heaps up in mounds, or even in cones. At a point where rocks come very near the surface, the water forms a chute above, strikes, and is shot up ten or fifteen feet, and piles back in gentle curves, as in a fountain; and on the river tumbles and rolls.

July 25.

Still more rapids and falls today. In one, the *Emma Dean* is caught in a whirlpool, and set spinning about; and it is with great difficulty we are able to get out of it, with the loss of an oar. At noon, another is made; and on we go, running some of the rapids, letting down with lines past others, and making two short portages. We camp on the right bank, hungry and tired.

July 26.

We run a short distance this morning, and go into camp, to make oars and repair boats and barometers. The walls of the canyon have been steadily increasing in altitude to this point, and now they are more than two thousand feet high. In many places, they are vertical from the water's edge; in others, there is a talus between the river and the foot of the cliffs, and they are often broken down by side canyons. It is probable that the river is nearly as low now as it is ever found. High water mark can be observed forty, fifty, sixty, or a hundred feet above its present stage. Sometimes logs and driftwood are seen wedged into the crevice overhead, where floods have carried them.

About ten o'clock, Powell, Bradley, Howland, Hall, and myself start up a side canyon to the east. We soon come to pools of water; then to a brook, which is lost in the sands below; and, passing up the brook, we find the canyon narrows, the walls close in, are often

[following page]
Tamarisks above granite rapids.

overhanging, and at last we find ourselves in a vast amphitheater, with a pool of deep, clear, cold water on the bottom. At first, our way seems cut off; but we soon discover a little shelf, along which we climb, and, passing beyond the pool, walk a hundred yards or more, turn to the right, and find ourselves in another dome-shaped amphitheater. There is a winding cleft at the top, reaching out to the country above, nearly two thousand feet overhead. The rounded, basin-shaped bottom is filled with water to the foot of the walls. There is no shelf by which we can pass around the foot. If we swim across, we meet with a face of rock hundreds of feet high, over which a little rill glides, and it will be impossible to climb. So we can go no farther up this canyon. Then we turn back, and examine the walls on either side carefully, to discover, if possible, some way of climbing out. In this search, every man takes his own course, and we are scattered. I almost abandon the idea of getting out, and am engaged in searching for fossils, when I discover, on the north, a broken place, up which it may be possible for me to climb. The way, for a distance, is up a slide of rocks; then up an irregular amphitheater, on points that form steps and give hand-hold, and then I reach a little shelf, along which I walk, and discover a vertical fissure, parallel to the face of the wall, and reaching to a higher shelf. This fissure is narrow, and I try to climb up to the bench, which is about forty feet overhead. I have a barometer on my back, which rather impedes my climbing. The walls of the fissure are of smooth limestone offering neither foot- nor hand-hold. So I support myself by pressing my back against one wall and my knees against the other, and, in this way, lift my body, in a shuffling manner, a few inches at a time, until I have, perhaps, made twenty-five feet of the distance, when the crevice widens a little, and I cannot press my knees against rocks in front with sufficient power to give me support in lifting my body, and I try to go back. This I cannot do without falling. So I struggle along sidewise, farther into the crevice, where it narrows. But by this time my muscles are exhausted, and I cannot climb longer; so I move still a little farther into the crevice, where it is so narrow and wedging that I can lie in it, and there I rest. Five or ten minutes of this relief, and up once more I go, and reach the bench above. On this I can walk for a quarter of a mile, till I come to a place where the wall is again broken down, so that I can climb up still farther, and in an hour I reach the summit. I hang up my barometer, to give it a few minutes time to settle, and occupy myself in collecting resin from the piñon pines, which are found in great abundance. One of the principal objects in making this climb was to get this resin, for the purpose of smearing our boats; but I have with me no means of carrying it down. The day is very hot, and my coat was left in camp, so I have no linings to tear out. Then it occurs to me to cut off the sleeve of my shirt, tie it up at one end, and in this little sack I collect about a gallon of pitch. After taking observations for altitude, I wander back on the rock, for an hour or two, when suddenly I notice that a storm is coming from the south. I seek a shelter in the rocks; but when the storm bursts, it comes down as a flood from the heavens, not with gentle drops at first, slowly increasing in quantity, but as if suddenly poured out. I am thoroughly drenched, and almost washed away. It lasts not more than half an hour, when the clouds sweep by to the north, and I have sunshine again.

In the meantime, I have discovered a better way of getting down, and I start for camp, making the greatest haste possible. On reaching the bottom of the side canyon, I find a thousand streams rolling down the cliffs on every side, carrying with them red sand; and these all unite in the canyon below, in one great stream of red mud.

Traveling as fast as I can run, I soon reach the foot of the stream, for the rain did not reach the lower end of the canyon, and the water is running down a dry bed of sand; and, although it comes in waves, several feet high and fifteen or twenty feet in width, the sands soak it up, and it is lost. But wave follows wave, and rolls along, and is swallowed up; and still the floods come on from above. I find that I can travel faster than the stream; so I hasten to camp, and tell the men there is a river coming down the canyon. We carry our camp equipage hastily from the bank, to where we think it will be above the water. Then we stand by, and see the river roll on to join the Colorado. Great quantities of gypsum are found at the bottom of the gorge; so we name it Gypsum Canyon.*

July 27.
We have more rapids and falls until noon; then we come to a narrow place in the canyon, with vertical walls for several hundred feet, above which are steep steps and sloping rocks back to the summits. The river is very narrow, and we make our way with great care and much anxiety, hugging the wall on the left . . .

* Named on 1871 trip—September 24.

Late in the afternoon, we pass to the left, around a sharp point, which is somewhat broken down near the foot, and discover a flock of mountain sheep on the rocks, more than a hundred feet above us. We quickly land in a cove, out of sight, and away go all the hunters with their guns, for the sheep have not discovered us. Soon, we hear firing, and those of us who have remained in the boats climb up to see what success the hunters have had. One sheep has been killed, and two of the men are still pursuing them. In a few minutes, we hear firing again, and the next moment down come the flock, clattering over the rocks, within twenty yards of us. One of the hunters seizes his gun, and brings a second sheep down, and the next minute the remainder of the flock is lost behind the rocks. We all give chase; but it is impossible to follow their tracks over the naked rock, and we see them no more. Where they went out of this rock-walled canyon is a mystery, for we can see no way of escape. Doubtless, if we could spare the time for the search, we could find some gulch up which they run.

We lash our prizes to the deck of one of the boats, and go on for a short distance; but fresh meat is too tempting for us, and we stop early to have a feast. And a feast it is! Two fine, young sheep. We care not for bread, or beans, or dried apples tonight; coffee and mutton is all we ask.

## July 28.

We make two portages this morning, one of them very long. During the afternoon we run a chute, more than half a mile in length, narrow and rapid. This chute has a floor of marble; the rocks dip in the direction in which we are going, and the fall of the stream conforms to the inclination of the beds; so we float on water that is gliding down an inclined plane. At the foot of the chute, the river turns sharply to the right, and the water rolls up against a rock which, from above, seems to stand directly athwart its course. As we approach it, we pull with all our power to the right, but it seems impossible to avoid being carried headlong against the cliff, and we are carried up high on the waves—not against the rocks, for the rebounding water strikes us, and we are beaten back and pass on with safety, except that we get a good drenching.

After this, the walls suddenly close in, so that the canyon is narrower than we have ever known it. The water fills it from wall to

Beyond the quiet dune swirl the furious rapids of the Upper Granite Gorge.

*" 'Bail!' shouted the Major,—'Bail for your lives!' and we dropped the oars to bail, though bailing was almost useless. . . . If you will take a watch and count by it ninety seconds, you will probably have about the time we were in this chaos, though it seemed much longer to me."*
— Frederich S. Dellenbaugh, member of the second (1871–72) Powell expedition.

wall, giving us no landing place at the foot of the cliff; the river is very swift, the canyon is very tortuous, so that we can see but a few hundred yards ahead; the walls tower over us, often overhanging so as to almost shut out the light. I stand on deck, watching with intensive anxiety, lest this may lead us into some danger; but we glide along, with no obstruction, no falls, no rocks, and, in a mile and a half, emerge from the narrow gorge into a more open and broken portion of the canyon. Now that it is past, it seems a very simple thing indeed to run through such a place, but the fear of what might be ahead made a deep impression on us.

At three o'clock we arrive at the foot of Cataract Canyon. Here a long canyon valley comes down from the east, and the river turns sharply to the west in a continuation of the line of the lateral valley. In the bend on the right, vast numbers of crags, and pinnacles, and tower-shaped rocks are seen. We call it Mille Crag Bend.

And now we wheel into another canyon, on swift water, unobstructed by rocks. This new canyon is very narrow and very straight, with walls vertical below and terraced above. The brink of the cliff is 1,300 feet above the water, where we enter it, but the rocks dip to the west, and, as the course of the canyon is in that direction, the walls are seen to slowly decrease in altitude. Floating down this narrow channel, and looking out through the canyon crevice away in the distance, the river is seen to turn again to the left, and beyond this point, away many miles, a great mountain is seen. Still floating down, we see other mountains, now to the right, now on the left, until a great mountain range is unfolded to view. We name this Narrow Canyon, and it terminates at the bend of the river below.

As we go down to this point, we discover the mouth of a stream, which enters from the right. Into this our little boat is turned. One of the men in the boat following, seeing what we have done, shouts to Dunn, asking if it is a trout-stream. Dunn replies, much disgusted, that it is "a dirty devil," and by this name the river is to be known hereafter. The water is exceedingly muddy, and has an unpleasant odor.

Some of us go out for half a mile, and climb a butte to the north. The course of the Dirty Devil River can be traced for many miles. It comes down through a very narrow canyon, and beyond it, to the southwest, there is a long line of cliffs, with a broad terrace, or bench, between it and the brink of the canyon, and beyond these

View across the Grand Canyon at Stone Creek.

*"Stand at some point on the brink of the Grand Canyon where you can overlook the river, and the details of the structure, the vast labyrinth of gorges of which it is composed, are scarcely noticed; the elements are lost in the grand effect, and a broad, deep flaring gorge of many colors is seen. But stand down among these gorges and the landscape seems to be composed of huge vertical elements of wonderful form. Above, it is an open, sunny gorge; below, it is deep and gloomy. Above, it is a chasm; below, it is a stairway from gloom to heaven."*
—John Wesley Powell

cliffs is situated the range of mountains seen as we came down Narrow Canyon.

Looking up the Colorado, the chasm through which it runs can be seen, but we cannot look down on its waters. The whole country is a region of naked rock, of many colors, with cliffs and buttes about us, and towering mountains in the distance.

July 29.

We enter a canyon today, with low, red walls. A short distance below its head we discover the ruins of an old building, on the left wall. There is a narrow plain between the river and the wall just here, and on the brink of a rock two hundred feet high stands an old house. Its walls are of stone, laid in mortar, with much regularity. It was probably built three stories high; the lower story is yet almost intact; the second is much broken down, and scarcely anything is left of the third. Great quantities of flint chips are found on the rocks near by, and many arrow heads, some perfect, others broken; and fragments of pottery are strewn about in great profusion. On the face of the cliff, under the building, and along down the river, for two or three hundred yards, there are many etchings. Two hours are given to the examination of these interesting ruins, then we run down fifteen miles farther, and discover another group. The principal building was situated on the summit of the hill. A part of the walls are standing, to the height of eight or ten feet, and the mortar yet remains, in some places. The house was in the shape of an L, with five rooms on the angle, and two in each extension. In the space in the angle, there is a deep excavation. From what we know of the people in the province of Tusayan, who are, doubtless, of the same race as the former inhabitants of these ruins, we conclude that this was a "kiva," or underground chamber, in which their religious ceremonies were performed.

We leave these ruins, and run down two or three miles, and go into camp about mid-afternoon. And now I climb the wall and go out into the back country for a walk.

The sandstone, through which the canyon is cut, is red and homogeneous, being the same as that through which Labyrinth Canyon runs. The smooth, naked rock stretches out on either side of the river for many miles, but curiously carved mounds and cones are scattered everywhere, and deep holes are worn out. Many of these pockets are filled with water. In one of these holes, or wells, twenty feet deep, I find a tree growing  The excavation is so narrow that I can step from its brink to a limb on the tree, and descend to the bottom of the well down a growing ladder. Many of these pockets are pot-holes, being found in the courses of little rills, or brooks, that run during the rains which occasionally fall in this region; and often a few harder rocks, which evidently assisted in their excavation, can be found in their bottoms. Others, which are shallower, are not so easily explained. Perhaps they are found where softer spots existed in the sandstone, places that yielded more readily to atmospheric degradation, and where the loose sands were carried away by the winds.

Just before sundown, I attempt to climb a rounded eminence, from which I hope to obtain a good outlook on the surrounding country. It is formed of smooth mounds, piled one above another. Up these I climb, winding here and there, to find a practicable way, until near the summit they become too steep for me to proceed. I search about, a few minutes, for a more easy way, when I am surprised at finding a stairway, evidently cut in the rock by hands. At one place, where there is a vertical wall of ten or twelve feet, I find an old, ricketty ladder. It may be that this was a watch-tower of that ancient people, whose home we have found in ruins. On many of the tributaries of the Colorado I have heretofore examined their deserted dwellings. Those that show evidences of being built during the latter part of their occupation of the country are, usually, placed on the most inaccessible cliffs. Sometimes, the mouths of caves have been walled across, and there are many other evidences to show their anxiety to secure defensible positions. Probably the nomadic tribes were sweeping down upon them, and they resorted to these cliffs and canyons for safety. It is not unreasonable to suppose that this orange mound was used as a watch-tower. Here I stand, where these now lost people stood centuries ago, and look over this strange country. I gaze off to great mountains, in the northwest, which are slowly covered by the night until they are lost, and then I return to camp. It is no easy task to find my way down the wall in the darkness, and I clamber about until it is nearly midnight, before I arrive.

July 30.
We make good progress today, as the water, though smooth, is swift. Sometimes, the canyon walls are vertical to the top; sometimes, they

are vertical below, and have a mound-covered slope above; in other places, the slope with its mounds, comes down to the water's edge.

Still proceeding on our way, we find the orange sandstone is cut in two by a group of firm, calcareous strata, and the lower bed is underlaid by soft gypsiferous shales. Sometimes, the upper homogeneous bed is a smooth, vertical wall, but usually it is carved with mounds, with gently meandering valley lines. The lower bed, yielding to gravity, as the softer shales below work out into the river, breaks into angular surfaces, often having a columnar appearance. One could almost imagine that the walls had been carved with a purpose, to represent giant architectual forms.

In the deep recesses of the walls, we find springs, with mosses and ferns on the moistened sandstone.

Glen Canyon.

July 31.

We have a cool, pleasant ride today, through this part of the canyon. The walls are steadily increasing in altitude, the curves are gentle, and often the river sweeps by an arc of vertical wall, smooth and unbroken, and then by a curve that is variegated by royal arches, mossy alcoves, deep, beautiful glens, and painted grottos.

Soon after dinner, we discover the mouth of the San Juan, where we camp. The remainder of the afternoon is given to hunting some way by which we can climb out of the canyon; but it ends in failure.

August 1.

We drop down two miles this morning, and go into camp again. There is a low, willow-covered strip of land along the walls on the east. Across this we walk, to explore an alcove which we see from the river. On entering, we find a little grove of box-elder and cottonwood trees; and, turning to the right, we find ourselves in a vast chamber, carved out of the rock. At the upper end there is a clear, deep pool of water, bordered with verdure. Standing by the side of this, we can see the grove at the entrance. The chamber is more than two hundred feet high, five hundred feet long, and two hundred feet wide. Through the ceiling, and on through the rocks for a thousand feet above, there is a narrow, winding skylight; and this is all carved out by a little stream, which only runs during the few showers that fall now and then in this arid country. The waters from the bare rocks back of the canyon, gathering rapidly into a

Stone Creek in the Grand Canyon.

small channel, have eroded a deep side canyon, through which they run, until they fall into the farther end of this chamber. The rock at the ceiling is hard, the rock below, very soft and friable; and, having cut through the upper harder portion down into the lower and softer, the stream has washed out these friable sandstones; and thus the chamber has been excavated.

Here we bring our camp. When "Old Shady" sings us a song at night, we are pleased to find that this hollow in the rock is filled with sweet sounds. It was doubtless made for an academy of music by its storm-born architect; so we name it Music Temple.

Music Temple, looking out.

August 2.

We still keep our camp in Music Temple today.

I wish to obtain a view of the adjacent country, if possible; so, early in the morning, the men take me across the river, and I pass along by the foot of the cliff half a mile up stream, and then climb first up broken ledges, then two or three hundred yards up a smooth, sloping rock, and then pass out on a narrow ridge. Still, I find I have not attained an altitude from which I can overlook the region outside of the canyon; and so I descend into a little gulch, and climb again to a higher ridge, all the way along naked sandstone, and at last I reach a point of commanding view. I can look several miles up the Sun Juan, and a long distance up the Colorado; and away to the northwest I can see the Henry Mountains*; to the northeast, the Sierra La Sal; to the southeast, unknown mountains; and to the southwest, the meandering of the canyon. Then I return to the bank of the river.

We sleep again in Music Temple.

August 3.

Start early this morning. The features of this canyon are greatly diversified. Still vertical walls at times. These are usually found to stand above great curves. The river, sweeping around these bends, undermines the cliffs in places. Sometimes, the rocks are overhanging; in other curves, curious, narrow glens are found. Through these we climb, by a rough stairway, perhaps several hundred feet, to where a spring bursts out from under an overhanging cliff, and where cottonwoods and willows stand, while, along the curves of

* Not named until later.

the brooklet, oaks grow, and other rich vegetation is seen, in marked contrast to the general appearance of naked rock. We call these Oak Glens.

Other wonderful features are the many side canyons or gorges that we pass. Sometimes, we stop to explore these for a short distance. In some places, their walls are much nearer each other above than below, so that they look somewhat like caves or chambers in the rocks. Usually, in going up such a gorge, we find beautiful vegetation; but our way is often cut off by deep basins, or pot-holes, as they are called.

On the walls, and back many miles into the country, numbers of monument-shaped buttes are observed. So we have a curious *ensemble* of wonderful features—carved walls, royal arches, glens, alcove gulches, mounds, and monuments. From which of these features shall we select a name? We decide to call it Glen Canyon.

Past these towering monuments, past these mounded billows of orange sandstone, past these oak-set glens, past these fern-decked alcoves, past these mural curves, we glide hour after hour, stopping now and then, as our attention is arrested by some new wonder, until we reach a point which is historic.

In the year 1776, Father Escalante, a Spanish priest, made an expedition from Santa Fé to the northwest, crossing the Grand and Green, and then passing down along the Wasatch Mountains and the southern plateaus, until he reached the Rio Virgen.* His intention was to cross to the Mission of Monterey; but, from information received from the Indians, he decided that the route was impracticable. Not wishing to return to Santa Fé over the circuitous route by which he had just traveled, he attempted to go by one more direct, and which led him across the Colorado, at a point known as *El vado de los Padres*.† From the description which we have read, we are enabled to determine the place. A little stream comes down through a very narrow side canyon from the west. It was down this that he came, and our boats are lying at the point where the ford crosses. A well-beaten Indian trail is seen here yet. Between the cliff and the river there is a little meadow. The ashes of many campfires are seen, and the bones of numbers of cattle are bleaching on the grass. For several years the Navajos have raided on the Mormons that dwell in

* Virgin River.

† Crossing of the Fathers.

the valleys to the west, and they doubtless cross frequently at this ford with their stolen cattle.

August 4.

Today the walls grow higher, and the canyon much narrower. Monuments are still seen on either side; beautiful glens, and alcoves, and gorges, and side canyons are yet found. After dinner, we find the river making a sudden turn to the northwest, and the whole character of the canyon changed. The walls are many hundreds of feet higher, and the rocks are chiefly variegated shales of beautiful colors— creamy orange above, then bright vermilion, and below, purple and chocolate beds, with green and yellow sands. We run four miles through this, in a direction a little to the west of north; wheel again to the west, and pass into a portion of the canyon where the characteristics are more like those above the bend. At night we stop at the mouth of a creek coming in from the right, and suppose it to be the Paria, which was described to me last year by a Mormon missionary.*

Here the canyon terminates abruptly in a line of cliffs, which stretches from either side across the river.

August 5.

With some feeling of anxiety, we enter a new canyon this morning. We have learned to closely observe the texture of the rock. In softer strata, we have a quiet river; in harder, we find rapids and falls. Below us are the limestones and hard sandstones, which we found in Cataract Canyon. This bodes toil and danger. Besides the texture of the rocks, there is another condition which affects the character of the channel, as we have found by experience. Where the strata are horizontal, the river is often quiet; but, even though it may be very swift in places, no great obstacles are found. Where the rocks incline in the direction traveled, the river usually sweeps with great velocity, but still we have few rapids and falls. But where the rocks dip up stream, and the river cuts obliquely across the upturned formations, harder strata above, and softer below, we have rapids and falls. Into hard rocks, and into rocks dipping up stream, we pass this morning, and start on a long, rocky, mad rapid. On the left there is a vertical rock, and down by this cliff and around to the left we glide, just tossed enough by the waves to appreciate the rate at which we are traveling.

* Bradley's diary indicates that Powell did not recognize the Paria at the time and that what Powell's (1869) diary calls Ute Creek was the Paria.

Granite dykes and schist.

99

The canyon is narrow, with vertical walls, which gradually grow higher. More rapids and falls are found. We come to one with a drop of sixteen feet, around which we make a portage, and then stop for dinner.

Then a run of two miles, and another portage, long and difficult; then we camp for the night, on a bank of sand.

August 6.

Canyon walls, still higher and higher, as we go down through strata. There is a steep talus at the foot of the cliff, and, in some places, the upper parts of the walls are terraced.

About ten o'clock we come to a place where the river occupies the entire channel, and the walls are vertical from the water's edge. We see a fall below, and row up against the cliff. There is a little shelf, or rather a horizontal crevice, a few feet over our heads. One man stands on the deck of the boat, another climbs on his shoulders, and then into the crevice. Then we pass him a line, and two or three others, with myself, follow; then we pass along the crevice until it becomes a shelf, as the upper part, or roof, is broken off. On this we walk for a short distance, slowly climbing all the way, until we reach a point where the shelf is broken off, and we can pass no farther. Then we go back to the boat, cross the stream, and get some logs that have lodged in the rocks, bring them to our side, pass them along the crevice and shelf, and bridge over the broken place. Then we go on to a point over the falls, but do not obtain a satisfactory view. Then we climb out to the top of the wall, and walk along to find a point below the fall, from which it can be seen. From this point it seems possible to let down our boats, with lines, to the head of the rapids, and then make a portage; so we return, row down by the side of the cliff, as far as we dare, and fasten one of the boats to a rock. Then we let down another boat to the end of its line beyond the first, and the third boat to the end of its line below the second, which brings it to the head of the fall, and under an overhanging rock. Then the upper boat, in obedience to a signal, lets go; we pull in the line, and catch the nearest boat as it comes, and then the last. Then we make a portage, and go on.

We go into camp early this afternoon, at a place where it seems possible to climb out, and the evening is spent in "making observations for time."

August 7.

The almanac tells us that we are to have an eclipse of the sun today, so Captain Powell and myself start early, taking our instruments with us, for the purpose of making observations on the eclipse, to determine our longitude. Arriving at the summit, after four hours' hard climbing, to attain 2,300 feet in height, we hurriedly build a platform of rocks, on which to place our instruments, and quietly wait for the eclipse; but clouds come on, and rain falls, and sun and moon are obscured.

Much disappointed, we start on our return to camp, but it is late, and the clouds make the night very dark. Still we feel our way down among the rocks with great care, for two or three hours, though making slow progress indeed. At last we lose our way, and dare proceed no farther. The rain comes down in torrents, and we can find no shelter. We can neither climb up nor go down, and in the darkness dare not move about, but sit and "weather out" the night.

August 8.

The limestone of this canyon is often polished, and makes a beautiful marble. Sometimes the rocks are of many colors—white, gray, pink, and purple, with saffron tints. It is with very great labor that we make progress, meeting with many obstructions, running rapids, letting down our boats with lines, from rock to rock, and sometimes carrying boats and cargoes around bad places. We camp at nght, just after a hard portage, under an overhanging wall, glad to find shelter from the rain. We have to search for some time to find a few sticks of driftwood, just sufficient to boil a cup of coffee.

The water sweeps rapidly in this elbow of river, and has cut its way under the rock, excavating a vast half circular chamber, which, if utilized for a theater, would give sitting to fifty thousand people. Objections might be raised against it, from the fact, at high water, the floor is covered with a raging flood.

August 9.

And now, the scenery is on a grand scale. The walls of the canyon, 2,500 feet high, are of marble of many beautiful colors, and often polished below by the waves, or far up the sides, where showers have washed the sands over the cliffs.

At one place I have a walk, for more than a mile, on a marble pavement, all polished and fretted with strange devices, and embossed in a thousand fantastic patterns. Through a cleft in the wall the sun shines on this pavement, which gleams in iridescent beauty.

I pass up into the cleft. It is very narrow, with a succession of pools standing at higher levels as I go back. The water in these pools is clear and cool, coming down from springs. Then I return to the pavement, which is but a terrace or bench, over which the river runs at its flood, but left bare at present. Along the pavement, in many places, are basins of clear water, in strange contrast to the red mud of the river. At length I come to the end of this marble terrace, and take again to the boat.

Riding down a short distance, a beautiful view is presented. The river turns sharply to the east, and seems inclosed by a wall, set with a million brilliant gems. What can it mean? Every eye is engaged, everyone wonders. On coming nearer, we find fountains bursting from the rock, high overhead, and the spray in the sunshine forms the gems which bedeck the wall. The rocks below the fountain are covered with mosses, and ferns, and many beautiful flowering plants. We name it Vasey's Paradise, in honor of the botanist who traveled with us last year.

We pass many side canyons today, that are dark, gloomy passages, back into the heart of the rocks that form the plateau through which this canyon is cut.

It rains again this afternoon. Scarcely do the first drops fall, when little rills run down the walls. As the storm comes on, the little rills increase in size, until great streams are formed. Although the walls of the canyon are chiefly limestone, the adjacent country is of red sandstone; and now the waters, loaded with these sands, come down in rivers of bright red mud, leaping over the walls in innumerable cascades. It is plain now how these walls are polished in many places.

At last, the storm ceases, and we go on. We have cut through the sandstones and limestones met in the upper part of the canyon, and through one great bed of marble a thousand feet in thickness. In this, great numbers of caves are hollowed out, and carvings are seen, which suggest architectural forms, though on a scale so grand that architectural terms belittle them. As this great bed forms a distinctive feature of the canyon, we call it Marble Canyon.

It is a peculiar feature of these walls, that many projections are set out into the river, as if the wall was buttressed for support. The walls themselves are half a mile high, and these buttresses are on a corresponding scale, jutting into the river scores of feet. In the recesses

Marble Canyon.

The 1871 *Emma Dean* with Major Powell's chair strapped on top.

Tapeats Creek emptying into the Grand Canyon.

between these projections there are quiet bays, except at the foot of a rapid, when they are dancing eddies or whirlpools. Sometimes these alcoves have caves at the back, giving them the appearance of great depth. Then other caves are seen above, forming vast, dome-shaped chambers. The walls, and buttresses, and chambers are all of marble.

The river is now quiet; the canyon wider. Above, when the river is at its flood, the waters gorge up, so that the difference between high and low water mark is often fifty or even seventy feet; but here, high water mark is not more than twenty feet above the present stage of the river. Sometimes there is a narrow flood-plain between the water and the wall.

Here we first discover *mesquite* shrubs, or small trees, with finely divided leaves and pods, somewhat like the locust.

The Colorado River.

August 10.

Walls still higher; water, swift again. We pass several broad, ragged canyons on our right, and up through these we catch glimpses of a forest-clad plateau, miles away to the west.

At two o'clock, we reach the mouth of the Colorado Chiquito.* This stream enters through a canyon, on a scale quite as grand as that of the Colorado itself. It is a very small river, and exceedingly muddy and salty. I walk up the stream three or four miles, this afternoon, crossing and recrossing where I can easily wade it. Then I climb several hundred feet at one place, and can see up the chasm, through which the river runs, for several miles. On my way back, I kill two rattlesnakes, and find, on my arrival, that another has been killed just at camp.

August 11.

We remain at this point today for the purpose of determining the latitude and longitude, measuring the height of the walls, drying our rations, and repairing our boats.

Captain Powell, early in the morning, takes a barometer, and goes out to climb a point between the two rivers.

I walk down the gorge to the left at the foot of the cliff, climb to a bench, and discover a trail, deeply worn in the rock. Where it crosses the side gulches, in some places, steps have been cut. I can see no evidence of its having been traveled for a long time. It was doubtless a path used by the people who inhabited this country anterior to the

* The Little Colorado.

Thunder River Falls above Tapeats Creek.

present Indian races—the people who built the communal houses, of which mention has been made.

I return to camp about three o'clock, and find that some of the men have discovered ruins, and many fragments of pottery; also, etchings and hieroglyphics on the rocks.

We find, tonight, on comparing the readings of the barometers, that the walls are about three thousand feet high—more than half a mile—an altitude difficult to appreciate from a mere statement of feet. The ascent is made, not by a slope such as is usually found in climbing a mountain, but is much more abrupt—often vertical for many hundreds of feet—so that the impression is that we are at great depths; and we look up to see but a little patch of sky.

Between the two streams, above the Colorado Chiquito, in some places the rocks are broken and shelving for six or seven hundred feet; then there is a sloping terrace, which can only be climbed by finding some way up a gulch; then, another terrace, and back, still another cliff. The summit of the cliff is three thousand feet above the river, as our barometers attest.

Our camp is below the Colorado Chiquito, and on the eastern side of the canyon.

The heart of Marble Canyon.

August 12.

The rocks above camp are rust-colored sandstones and conglomerates. Some are very hard; others quite soft. These all lie nearly horizontal, and the beds of softer material have been washed out, and left the harder, thus forming a series of shelves. Long lines of these are seen, of varying thickness, from one or two to twenty or thirty feet, and the spaces between have the same variability. This morning, I spend two or three hours in climbing among these shelves, and then I pass above them, and go up a long slope, to the foot of the cliff, and try to discover some way by which I can reach the top of the wall; but I find my progress cut off by an amphitheater. Then, I wander away around to the left, up a little gulch, and along benches, and climb, from time to time, until I reach an altitude of nearly two thousand feet, and can get no higher. From this point, I can look off to the west, up side canyons of the Colorado, and see the edge of a great plateau, from which streams run down into the Colorado, and deep gulches, in the escarpment which faces us, continued by canyons, ragged and flaring, and set with cliffs and towering crags, down to the river. I can see far up

Towers of the Vermilion Cliffs.

Marble Canyon, to long lines of chocolate-colored cliffs, and above these, the Vermilion Cliffs. I can see, also, up the Colorado Chiquito, through a very ragged and broken canyon, with sharp salients set out from the walls on either side, their points overlapping, so that a huge tooth of marble, on one side, seems to be set between two teeth on the opposite; and I can also get glimpses of walls, standing away back from the river, while over my head are mural escarpments, not possible to be scaled.

# The Grand Canyon of the Colorado

August 13.

We are now ready to start on our way down the Great Unknown. Our boats, tied to a common stake, are chafing each other, as they are tossed by the fretful river. They ride high and buoyant, for their loads are lighter than we could desire. We have but a month's rations remaining. The flour has been resifted through the mosquito-net sieve; the spoiled bacon has been dried, and the worst of it boiled; the few pounds of dried apples have been spread in the sun, and reshrunken to their normal bulk; the sugar has all melted, and gone on its way down the river; but we have a large sack of coffee. The lighting of the boats has this advantage: they will ride the waves better, and we shall have but little to carry when we make a portage

We are three-quarters of a mile in the depths of the earth, and the great river shrinks into insignificance, as it dashes its angry waves

[following page]
Running the granite rapids in today's pontoon boats is safer than it was for Powell's party, yet the course steered is frequently uncertain. Dellenbaugh leaves us this account of the second expedition:

*"At times we could barely maintain control of the boats so powerful and uninterrupted was the turbulent sweep of the great narrow flood. At one place as we were being hurled along at a tremendous speed we suddenly perceived immediately ahead of us and in such a position that we could not avoid dashing into it, a fearful commotion of the waters, indicating many large rocks near the surface. The Major stood on the middle deck, his life-preserver in place, and holding by his left hand to the arm of the well-secured chair to prevent being thrown off by the lurching of the boat, peered into the approaching maelstrom. It looked to him like the end for us and he exclaimed calmly, 'By God, boys, we're gone!' With terrific impetus we sped into the seething, boiling turmoil, expecting to feel a crash and to have the* Dean *crumble beneath us, but instead of that unfortunate result she shot through smoothly without a scratch, the rocks being deeper than appeared by the disturbance on the surface. We had no time to think over this agreeable delivery, for on came the rapids or rather other rough portions of the unending declivity requiring instant and continuous attention, the Major rapidly giving the orders, Left, right, hard on the right, steady, hard on the left,* hard on the left, H-A-R-D ON THE LEFT, *pull away strong."*

against the walls and cliffs, that rise to the world above; they are but puny ripples, and we but pigmies, running up and down the sands, or lost among the boulders.

We have an unknown distance yet to run; an unknown river yet to explore. What falls there are, we know not; what rocks beset the channel, we know not; what walls rise over the river, we know not. Ah, well! we may conjecture many things. The men talk as cheerfully* as ever; jests are bandied about freely this morning; but to me the cheer is somber and the jests are ghastly.

With some eagerness, and some anxiety, and some misgiving, we enter the canyon below, and are carried along by the swift water through walls which rise from its very edge. They have the same structure as we noticed yesterday—tiers of irregular shelves below, and above these, steep slopes to the foot of marble cliffs. We run six miles in a little more than half an hour, and emerge into a more open portion of the canyon, where high hills and ledges of rock intervene between the river and the distant walls. Just at the head of this open place the river runs across a dike; that is, a fissure in the rocks, open to depths below, has been filled with eruptive matter, and this, on cooling, was harder than the rocks through which the crevice was made, and, when these were washed away, the harder volcanic matter remained as a wall, and the river has cut a gateway through it several hundred feet high, and as many wide. As it crosses the wall, there is a fall below, and a bad rapid, filled with boulders of trap; so we stop to make a portage. Then on we go, gliding by hills and ledges, with distant walls in view; sweeping past sharp angles of rock; stopping at a few points to examine rapids, which we find can be run, until we have made another five miles, when we land for dinner.

Then we let down with lines, over a long rapid, and start again. Once more the walls close in, and we find ourselves in a narrow gorge, the water again filling the channel, and very swift. With great care, and constant watchfulness, we proceed, making about four miles this afternoon, and camp in a cave.

August 14.

At daybreak we walk down the bank of the river, on a little sandy beach, to take a view of a new feature in the canyon. Heretofore, hard rocks have given us bad river; soft rocks, smooth water; and a series

* Bradley's diary would indicate the opposite.

Head of the Grand Canyon.

The Grand Canyon looking east.

of rocks harder than any we have experienced sets in. The river enters the granite!*

We can see but a little way into the granite gorge, but it looks threatening.

After breakfast we enter on the waves. At the very introduction, it inspires awe. The canyon is narrower than we have ever before seen it; the water is swifter; there are but few broken rocks in the channel; but the walls are set, on either side, with pinnacles and crags; and sharp, angular buttresses, bristling with wind and wave polished spires, extend far out into the river.

Ledges of rocks jut into the stream, their tops sometimes just below the surface, sometimes rising few or many feet above; and island ledges, and island pinnacles, and island towers break the swift course of the stream into chutes, and eddies, and whirlpools. We soon reach a place where a creek comes in from the left, and just below, the channel is choked with boulders, which have washed down this lateral canyon and formed a dam, over which there is a fall of thirty or forty feet; but on the boulders we can get foothold, and we make a portage.

Three more such dams are found. Over one we make a portage; at the other two we find chutes, through which we can run.

As we proceed, the granite rises higher, until nearly a thousand feet of the lower part of the walls are composed of this rock.

About eleven o'clock we hear a great roar ahead, and approach it very cautiously. The sound grows louder and louder as we run, and at last we find ourselves above a long, broken fall, with ledges and pinnacles of rock obstructing the river. There is a descent of, perhaps, seventy-five or eighty feet in a third of a mile, and the rushing waters break into great waves on the rocks, and lash themselves into a mad, white foam. We can land just above, but there is no foothold on either side by which we can make a portage. It is nearly a thousand feet to the top of the granite, so it will be impossible to carry our boats around, though we can climb to the summit up a side gulch, and, passing along a mile or two, can descend to the river. This we find on examination; but such a portage would be impracticable for us, and we must run the rapid, or abandon the river. There is no hesitation. We step into our boats, push off and away we go, first on smooth but swift water, then we strike a glassy wave, and ride to its top, down again into the trough, up again

Grand Canyon looking east at Toroweap, Arizona.

* Geologists would call these rocks metamorphic crystalline schists, with dikes and beds of granite, but we will use the popular name for the whole series—granite.

on a higher wave, and down and up on waves higher and still higher, until we strike one just as it curls back, and a breaker rolls over our little boat. Still, on we speed, shooting past projecting rocks, till the little boat is caught in a whirlpool, and spun around several times. At last we pull out again into the stream, and now the other boats have passed us. The open compartment of the *Emma Dean* is filled with water, and every breaker rolls over us. Hurled back from a rock, now on this side, now on that, we are carried into an eddy, in which we struggle for a few minutes, and are then out again, the breakers still rolling over us. Our boat is unmanageable, but she cannot sink, and we drift down another hundred yards, through breakers; how, we scarcely know. We find the other boats have turned into an eddy at the foot of the fall, and are waiting to catch us as we come, for the men have seen that our boat is swamped. They push out as we come near, and pull us in against the wall. We bail our boat, and on we go again.

The walls, now, are more than a mile in height—a vertical distance difficult to appreciate. Stand on the south steps of the Treasury building, in Washington, and look down Pennsylvania Avenue to the Capitol Park, and measure this distance overhead, and imagine cliffs to extend to that altitude, and you will understand what I mean; or, stand at Canal street, in New York and look up Broadway to Grace Church, and you have about the distance; or, stand at Lake street bridge, in Chicago, and look down to the Central Depot, and you have it again.

A thousand feet of this is up through granite crags, then steep slopes and perpendicular cliffs rise, one above another, to the summit. The gorge is black and narrow below, red and gray and flaring above, with crags and angular projections on the walls, which, cut in many places by side canyons, seem to be a vast wilderness of rocks. Down in these grand, gloomy depths we glide, ever listening, for the mad waters keep up their roar; ever watching, ever peering ahead, for the narrow canyon is winding, and the river is closed in so that we can see but a few hundred yards, and what there may be below we know not; but we listen for falls, and watch for rocks, or stop now and then, in the bay of a recess, to admire the gigantic scenery. And ever, as we go, there is some new pinnacle or tower, some crag or peak, some distant view of the upper plateau, some strange-shaped rock, or some deep, narrow side canyon. Then we come to another broken fall, which appears more difficult than the one we ran this morning.

A small creek comes in on the right, and the first fall of the water

At the mouth of the Little Colorado where the big river turns brown from the desert runoff above.

The Inner Gorge.

Looking down Deer Creek.

is over boulders, which have been carried down by this lateral stream. We land at its mouth, and stop for an hour or two to examine the fall. It seems possible to let down with lines, at least a part of the way, from point to point, along the right-hand wall. So we make a portage over the first rocks, and find footing on some boulders below. Then we let down one of the boats to the end of her line, when she reaches a corner of the projecting rock, to which one of the men clings, and steadies her, while I examine an eddy below. I think we can pass the other boats down by us, and catch them in the eddy. This is soon done and the men in the boats in the eddy pull us to their side. On the shore of this little eddy there is about two feet of gravel beach above the water. Standing on this beach, some of the men take the line of the little boat and let it drift down against another projecting angle. Here is a little shelf, on which a man from my boat climbs, and a shorter line is passed to him, and he fastens the boat to the side of the cliff. Then the second one is let down, bringing the line of the third. When the second boat is tied up, the two men standing on the beach above spring into the last boat, which is pulled up alongside of ours. Then we let down the boats, for twenty-five or thirty yards, by walking along the shelf, landing them again in the mouth of a side canyon. Just below this there is another pile of boulders, over which we make another portage. From the foot of these rocks we can climb to another shelf, forty or fifty feet above the water.

On this bench we camp for the night. We find a few sticks, which have lodged in the rocks. It is raining hard, and we have no shelter, but kindle a fire and have our supper. We sit on the rocks all night, wrapped in our ponchos, getting what sleep we can.

Reeds at Deer Creek.

August 15.

This morning we find we can let down for three or four hundred yards, and it is managed in this way: We pass along the wall, by climbing from projecting point to point, sometimes near the water's edge, at other places fifty or sixty feet above, and hold the boat with a line, while two men remain aboard, and prevent her from being dashed against the rocks, and keep the line from getting caught on the wall. In two hours we had brought them all down, as far as it is possible, in this way. A few yards below, the river strikes with great violence against a projecting rock, and our boats are pulled up in a little bay above. We must now manage to pull out of this, and clear the point below. The little boat is held by the bow obliquely up the stream. We jump in, and pull out only a few strokes, and sweep clear of the dangerous rock. The other boats follow in the same manner, and the rapid is passed.

It is not easy to describe the labor of such navigation. We must prevent the waves from dashing the boats against the cliffs. Sometimes, where the river is swift, we must put a bight of rope around a rock, to prevent her being snatched from us by a wave; but where the plunge is too great, or the chute too swift, we must let her leap, and catch her below, or the undertow will drag her under the falling water, and she sinks. Where we wish to run her out a little way from shore, through a channel between rocks, we first throw in little sticks of driftwood, and watch their course, to see where we must steer, so that she will pass the channel in safety. And so we hold, and let go, and pull, and lift, and ward, among rocks, around rocks, and over rocks.

And now we go on through this solemn, mysterious way. The river is very deep, the canyon very narrow, and still obstructed, so that there is no steady flow of the stream; but the waters wheel, and roll, and boil, and we are scarcely able to determine where we can go. Now, the boat is carried to the right, perhaps close to the wall; again, she is shot into the stream, and perhaps is dragged over to the other side, where, caught in a whirlpool, she spins about. We can neither land nor run as we please. The boats are entirely unmanageable; no order in their running can be preserved; now one, now another, is ahead, each crew laboring for its own preservation. In such a place we come to another rapid. Two of the boats run it perforce. One succeeds in landing, but there is no foothold by which to make a portage, and she is pushed out again into the stream. The next minute a great reflex wave fills the open compartment; she is water-logged, and drifts unmanageable. Breaker after breaker rolls over her, and one capsizes her. The men are thrown out; but they cling to the boat, and she drifts down some distance, alongside of us, and we are able to catch her. She is soon bailed out, and the men are aboard once more; but the oars are lost, so a pair from the *Emma Dean* is spared. Then for two miles we find smooth water.

Clouds are playing in the canyon today. Sometimes they roll down in great masses, filling the gorge with gloom; sometimes they hang above, from wall to wall, and cover the canyon with a roof of impending storm; and we can peer long distances up and down this canyon corridor, with its cloud roof overhead, its walls of black granite, and its river bright with the sheen of broken waters. Then, a gust of wind sweeps down a side gulch, and, making a rift in the clouds, reveals the blue heavens, and a stream of sunlight pours in. Then, the clouds drift away into the distance, and hang around crags, and peaks, and pinnacles, and towers, and walls, and cover them with a mantle, that lifts from time to time, and sets them all in sharp relief. Then, baby clouds creep out of side canyons, glide around points, and creep back again, into more distant gorges. Then, clouds, set in strata, cross the canyon, with intervening vista views, to cliffs and rocks beyond. The clouds are children of the heavens, and when they play among the rocks, they lift them to the region above.

It rains! Rapidly little rills are formed above, and these soon grow into brooks, and the brooks grow into creeks, and tumble over the walls in innumerable cascades, adding their wild music to the roar of the river. When the rain ceases, the rills, brooks, and creeks run dry. The waters that fall, during a rain, on these steep rocks, are gathered at once into the river; they could scarcely be poured in more suddenly, if some vast spout ran from the clouds to the stream itself. When a storm bursts over the canyon, a side gulch is dangerous, for a sudden flow may come, and the inpouring waters will raise the river, so as to hide the rocks before your eyes.

Early in the afternoon, we discover a stream, entering from the north, a clear, beautiful creek, coming down through a gorgeous red canyon. We land, and camp on a sand beach, above its mouth, under a great, overspreading tree, with willow-shaped leaves.

August 16.

We must dry our rations again today, and make oars.

A gable with pinnacles.

The Colorado is never a clear stream, but for the past three or four days it has been raining much of the time, and the floods, which are poured over the walls, have brought down great quantities of mud, making it exceedingly turbid now. The little affluent, which we have discovered here, is a clear, beautiful creek, or river, as it would be termed in this western country, where streams are not abundant. We have named one stream, away above, in honor of the great chief of the "Bad Angels," and, as this is in beautiful contrast to that, we conclude to name it "Bright Angel."*

Early in the morning, the whole party starts up to explore the Bright

* Powell did not coin this name until December 1869, when he used it on the lecture platform to contrast with "Dirty Devil."

Angel River, with the special purpose of seeking timber, from which to make oars. A couple of miles above, we find a large pine log, which has been floated down from the plateau, probably from an altitude of more than six thousand feet, but not many miles back. On its way, it must have passed over many cataracts and falls, for it bears scars in evidence of the rough usage which it has received. The men roll it on skids, and the work of sawing oars is commenced.

This stream heads away back, under a line of abrupt cliffs, that terminates the plateau, and tumbles down more than four thousand feet in the first mile or two of its course; then runs through a deep, narrow canyon, until it reaches the river.

Late in the afternoon I return, and go up a little gulch, just above this creek, about two hundred yards from camp, and discover the ruins of two or three old houses, which were originally of stone, laid in mortar. Only the foundations are left, but irregular blocks, of which the houses were constructed, lie scattered about. In one room I find an old mealing stone, deeply worn, as if it had been much used. A great deal of pottery is strewn around, and old trails, which in some places are deeply worn into the rocks, are seen.

It is ever a source of wonder to us why these ancient people sought such inaccessible places for their homes. They were, doubtless, an agricultural race, but there are no lands here, of any considerable extent, that they could have cultivated. To the west of Oraiby, one of the towns in the "Province of Tusayan," in Northern Arizona, the inhabitants have actually built little terraces along the face of the cliff, where a spring gushes out, and thus made their sites for gardens. It is possible that the ancient inhabitants of this place made their agricultural lands in the same way. But why should they seek such spots? Surely, the country was not so crowded with population as to demand the utilization of so barren a region. The only solution of the problem suggested is this: We know that, for a century or two after the settlement of Mexico, many expeditions were sent into the country, now comprised in Arizona and New Mexico, for the purpose of bringing the town-building people under the dominion of the Spanish government. Many of their villages were destroyed, and the inhabitants fled to regions at that time unknown; and there are traditions, among the people who inhabit the *pueblos* that still remain, that the canyons were these unknown lands. Maybe these buildings were erected at that time; sure it is that they have a much more modern appearance than the ruins scattered

Deer Creek: View into chasm.

118

over Nevada, Utah, Colorado, Arizona, and New Mexico. Those old Spanish conquerors had a monstrous greed for gold, and a wonderful lust for saving souls. Treasures they must have; if not on earth, why, then, in heaven; and when they failed to find heathen temples, bedecked with silver, they propitiated Heaven by seizing the heathen themselves. There is yet extant a copy of a record, made by a heathen artist, to express his conception of the demands of the conquerors. In one part of the picture we have a lake, and near by stands a priest pouring water on the head of a native. On the other side, a poor Indian has a cord about his throat. Lines run from these two groups, to a central figure, a man with beard, and full Spanish panoply. The interpretation of the picture writing is this: "Be baptized, as this saved heathen; or be hanged, as that damned heathen." Doubtless, some of these people preferred a third alternative, and, rather than be baptized or hanged, they chose to be imprisoned within these canyon walls.

August 17.

Our rations are still spoiling; the bacon is so badly injured that we are compelled to throw it away. By an accident, this morning, the saleratus is lost overboard. We have now only musty flour sufficient for ten days, a few dried apples, but plenty of coffee. We must make all haste possible. If we meet with difficulties, as we have done in the canyon above, we may be compelled to give up the expedition, and try to reach the Mormon settlements to the north. Our hopes are that the worst places are passed, but our barometers are all so much injured as to be useless, so we have lost our reckoning in altitude, and know not how much descent the river has yet to make.

The stream is still wild and rapid, and rolls through a narrow channel. We make but slow progress, often landing against a wall, and climbing around some point, where we can see the river below. Although very anxious to advance, we are determined to run with great caution, lest, by another accident, we lose all our supplies. How precious that little flour has become! We divide it among the boats, and carefully store it away, so that it can be lost only by the loss of the boat itself.

We make ten miles and a half, and camp among the rocks, on the right. We have had rain, from time to time, all day, and have been thoroughly drenched and chilled; but between showers the sun shines with great power, and the mercury in our thermometers stands at 115°, so that we have rapid changes from great extremes, which are very disagreeable. It is especially cold in the rain tonight. The little canvas we have is rotten and useless; the rubber ponchos, with which we started from Green River City, have all been lost; more than half the party is without hats, and not one of us has an entire suit of clothes, and we have not a blanket apiece. So we gather driftwood, and build a fire; but after supper the rain, coming down in torrents, extinguishes it, and we sit up all night, on the rocks, shivering, and are more exhausted by the night's discomfort than by the day's toil.

August 18.
The day is employed in making portages, and we advance but two miles on our journey. Still it rains.

While the men are at work making portages, I climb up the granite to its summit, and go away back over the rust-colored sandstones and greenish-yellow shales, to the foot of the marble wall. I climb so high that the men and boats are lost in the black depths below, and the dashing river is a rippling brook; and still there is more canyon above than below. All about me are interesting geological records. The book is open, and I can read as I run. All about me are grand views, for the clouds are playing again in the gorges. But somehow I think of the nine days' rations, and the bad river, and the lesson of the rocks, and the glory of the scene is but half seen.

I push on to an angle, where I hope to get a view of the country beyond, to see, if possible, what the prospect may be of our soon running through this plateau, or at least of meeting with some geological change that will let us out of the granite; but, arriving at the point, I can see below only a labyrinth of deep gorges.

August 19.
Rain again this morning. Still we are in our granite prison, and the time is occupied until noon in making a long, bad portage.

After dinner, in running a rapid, the pioneer boat is upset by a wave. We are some distance in advance of the larger boats, the river is rough and swift, and we are unable to land, but cling to the boat, and are carried down stream, over another rapid. The men in the boats above see our trouble, but they are caught in whirlpools, and are spinning about in eddies, and it seems a long time before they come to our relief. At last they do come; our boat is turned right side up, bailed out; the oars, which fortunately have floated along in company with us, are gathered up, and on we go, without even landing.

A side canyon near Surprise Valley.

Soon after the accident the clouds break away, and we have sunshine again.

Soon we find a little beach, with just room enough to land. Here we camp, but there is no wood. Across the river, and a little way above, we see some driftwood lodged in the rocks. So we bring two boat loads over, build a huge fire, and spread everything to dry. It is the first cheerful night we have had for a week; a warm, drying fire in the midst of the camp, and a few bright stars in our patch of heavens overhead.

August 20.

The characteristics of the canyon change this morning. The river is broader, the walls more sloping and composed of black slate, and stand on edge. These nearly vertical slates are washed out in places—that is, the softer beds are washed out between the harder, which are left standing. In this way, curious little alcoves are formed, in which are quiet bays of water, but on a much smaller scale than the great bays and buttresses of Marble Canyon.

The river is still rapid, and we stop to let down with lines several times, but make greater progress as we run ten miles. We camp on the right bank. Here, on a terrace of trap, we discover another group of ruins. There was evidently quite a village on this rock. Again we find mealing stones, and much broken pottery, and up in a little natural shelf in the rock, back of the ruins, we find a globular basket, that would hold perhaps a third of a bushel. It is badly broken, and, as I attempt to take it up, it falls to pieces. There are many beautiful flint chips, as if this had been the home of an old arrow maker.

August 21.

We start early this morning, cheered by the prospect of a fine day, and encouraged, also, by the good run made yesterday. A quarter of a mile below camp the river turns abruptly to the left, and between camp and that point is very swift, running down in a long, broken chute, and piling up against the foot of the cliff, where it turns to the left. We try to pull across, so as to go down on the other side, but the waters are swift, and it seems impossible for us to escape the rock below; but, in pulling across, the bow of the boat is turned to the farther shore, so that we are swept broadside down, and are prevented, by the rebounding waters, from striking against the wall. There we toss about for a few seconds in these billows, and are carried past the danger. Below, the

Elves Cavern.

river turns again to the right, the canyon is very narrow, and we see in advance but a short distance. The water, too, is very swift, and there is no landing-place. From around this curve there comes a mad roar, and down we are carried, with a dizzying velocity, to the head of another rapid. On either side, high over our heads, there are overhanging granite walls, and the sharp bends cut off our view, so that a few minutes will carry us into unknown waters. Away we go, on one long, winding chute. I stand on deck, supporting myself with a strap, fastened on either side to the gunwale, and the boat glides rapidly, where the water is smooth, or, striking a wave, she leaps and bounds like a thing of life, and we have a wild, exhilarating ride for ten miles, which we make in less than an hour. The excitement is so great that we forget the danger, until we hear the roar of a great fall below; then we back on our oars, and are carried slowly toward its head, and succeed in landing just above, and find that we have to make another portage. At this we are engaged until some time after dinner.

Just here we run out of the granite!

Ten miles in less than half a day, and limestone walls below. Good cheer returns; we forget the storms, and gloom, and cloud-covered canyons, and the black granite, and the raging river, and push our boats from shore in great glee.

Though we are out of the granite, the river is still swift, and we wheel about a point again to the right, and turn, so as to head back in the direction from which we come, and see the granite again, with its narrow gorge and black crags; but we meet with no more great falls, or rapids. Still, we run cautiously, and stop, from time to time, to examine some places which look bad. Yet, we make ten miles this afternoon; twenty miles, in all, today.

August 22.

We come to rapids again, this morning, and are occupied several hours in passing them, letting the boats down, from the rock to rock, with lines, for nearly half a mile, and then have to make a long portage. While the men are engaged in this, I climb the wall on the northeast, to a height of about two thousand five hundred feet, where I can obtain a good view of a long stretch of canyon below Its course is to the southwest. The walls seem to rise very abruptly, for two thousand five hundred or three thousand feet, and then there is a gently sloping terrace, on each side, for two or three miles, and again we find cliffs, one

Kanab Canyon, near junction of the Green and Colorado (then called Grand) rivers.

An alcove in the Red Wall.

thousand five hundred or two thousand feet high. From the brink of these the plateau stretches back to the north and south, for a long distance. Away down the canyon, on the right wall, I can see a group of mountains, some of which appear to stand on the brink of the canyon. The effect of the terrace is to give the appearance of a narrow winding valley, with high walls on either side, and a deep, dark, meandering gorge down its middle. It is impossible, from this point of view, to determine whether we have granite at the bottom, or not; but, from geological considerations, I conclude that we shall have marble walls below.

After my return to the boats, we run another mile, and camp for the night.

We have made but little over seven miles today, and a part of our flour has been soaked in the river again.

August 23.

Our way today is again through marble walls. Now and then, we pass, for a short distance, through pitches of granite, like hills thrust up into the limestone. At one of these places we have to make another portage, and, taking advantage of the delay, I go up a little stream, to the north, wading it all the way, sometimes having to plunge in to my neck; in other places being compelled to swim across little basins that have been excavated at the foot of the falls. Along its course are many cascades and springs gushing out from the rocks on either side. Sometimes a cottonwood tree grows over the water. I come to one beautiful fall, of more than a hundred and fifty feet, and climb around it to the right, on the broken rocks. Still going up, I find the canyon narrowing very much, being but fifteen or twenty feet wide; yet the walls rise on either side many hundreds of feet, perhaps thousands; I can hardly tell.

In some places the stream has not excavated its channel down vertically through the rocks, but has cut obliquely, so that one wall overhangs the other. In other places it is cut vertically above and obliquely below, or obliquely above and vertically below, so that it is impossible to see out overhead. But I can go no farther. The time which I estimated it would take to make the portage has almost expired, and I start back on a round trot, wading in the creek where I must, and plunging through basins, and find the men waiting for me, and away we go on the river.

Just after dinner we pass a stream on the right, which leaps into the Colorado by a direct fall of more than a hundred feet, forming a beautiful cascade. There is a bed of very hard rock above, thirty or forty feet in thickness, and much softer beds below. The hard beds above project many yards beyond the softer, which are washed out, forming a deep cave behind the fall, and the stream pours through a narrow crevice above into a deep pool below. Around on the rocks, in the cave-like chamber, are set beautiful ferns, with delicate fronds and enameled stalks. The little frondlets have their points turned down, to form spore cases. It has very much the appearance of the Maiden's Hair fern, but is much larger. This delicate foliage covers the rocks all about the fountain, and gives the chamber great beauty. But we have little time to spend in admiration, so on we go.

We make fine progress this afternoon, carried along by a swift river, and shoot over the rapids, finding no serious obstructions.

The canyon walls, for two thousand five hundred or three thousand feet, are very regular, rising almost perpendicularly, but here and there set with narrow steps, and occasionally we can see away above the broad terrace, to distant cliffs.

We camp tonight in a marble cave, and find, on looking at our reckoning, we havet run twenty-two miles.

August 24.

The canyon is wider today. The walls rise to a vertical height of nearly three thousand feet. In many places the river runs under a cliff, in great curves, forming amphitheaters, half-dome shaped.

The waterfall in Elves Cavern.

Though the river is rapid, we meet with no serious obstructions, and run twenty miles. It is curious how anxious we are to make up our reckoning every time we stop, now that our diet is confined to plenty of coffee, very little spoiled flour, and very few dried apples. It has come to be a race for a dinner. Still, we make such fine progress, all hands are in good cheer, but not a moment of daylight is lost.

August 25.

We make twelve miles this morning, when we come to monuments of lava, standing in the river; low rocks, mostly, but some of them shafts more than a hundred feet high. Going on down, three or four miles, we find them increasing in number. Great quantities of cooled lava and many cinder-cones are seen on either side; and then we come to an abrupt cataract. Just over the fall, on the right wall, a cinder-cone, or extinct volcano, with a well-defined crater, stands on the very brink of the canyon. This, doubtless, is the one we saw two or three days ago. From this volcano vast floods of lava have been poured down into the river, and a stream of the molten rock has run up the canyon, three or four miles, and down, we know not how far. Just where it poured over the canyon wall is the fall. The whole north side, as far as we can see, is lined with the black basalt, and high up on the opposite wall are patches of the same material, resting on the benches, and filling old alcoves and caves, giving to the wall a spotted appearance.

The rocks are broken in two, along a line which here crosses the river, and the beds, which we have seen coming down the canyon for the last thirty miles, have dropped 800 feet, on the lower side of the line, forming what geologists call a fault. The volcanic cone stands directly over the fissure thus formed. On the side of the river opposite, mammoth springs burst out of this crevice, one or two hundred feet above the river, pouring in a stream quite equal in volume to the Colorado Chiquito.

Grapevines in Kanab Creek.

This stream seems to be loaded with carbonate of lime, and the water, evaporating, leaves an incrustation on the rocks; and this process has been continued for a long time, for extensive deposits are noticed, in which are basins, with bubbling springs. The water is salty.

We have to make a portage here, which is completed in about three hours, and on we go.

This is how Lava Falls looked
to John Wesley Powell.

Cottonwood trees growing in Lava Canyon.

Today's canyoneers battling the rapids.

Looking across Lava Falls in the 1870's.

Lava boulders.

We have no difficulty as we float along, and I am able to observe the wonderful phenomena connected with this flood of lava. The canyon was doubtless filled to a height of twelve or fifteen hundred feet, perhaps by more than one flood. This would dam the water back; and in cutting through this great lava bed, a new channel has been formed, sometimes on one side, sometimes on the other. The cooled lava being of firmer texture than the rocks of which the walls are composed, remains in some places; in others a narrow channel has been cut, leaving a line of basalt on either side. It is possible that the lava cooled faster on the sides against the walls, and that the center ran out; but of this we can only conjecture. There are other places, where almost the whole of the lava is gone, patches of it only being seen where it has caught on the walls. As we float down, we can see that it ran out into side canyons. In some places this has a fine, columnar structure, often in concentric prisms, and masses of these concentric columns have coalesced. In some places, when the flow occurred, the canyon was probably at about the same depth as it is now, for we can see where the basalt has rolled out on the sands, and, what seems serious to me, the sands are not melted or metamorphosed to any appreciable extent. In places the bed of the river is of sandstone or limestone, in other places of lava, showing that it has all been cut out again where the sandstones and limestones appear; but there is a little yet left where the bed is of lava.

What a conflict of water and fire there must have been here! Just imagine a river of molten rock, running down into a river of melted snow. What a seething and boiling of the waters; what clouds of steam rolled into the heavens!

Thirty-five miles today. Hurrah!

August 26.

The canyon walls are steadily becoming higher as we advance. They are still bold, and nearly vertical up to the terrace. We still see evidence of the eruption discovered yesterday, but the thickness of the basalt is decreasing, as we go down the stream; yet it has been reinforced at points by streams that have come down from volcanoes standing on the terrace above, but which we cannot see from the river below.

Since we left the Colorado Chiquito, we have seen no evidences that the tribe of Indians inhabiting the plateaus on either side ever

[following page]
Granite-schist formations near Redrock Canyon.

*"Each wall of the canyon is a composite structure, a wall composed of many walls, but never a repetition. Every one of these almost innumerable gorges is a world of beauty in itself. In the Grand Canyon there are thousands of gorges like that below Niagara Falls, and there are a thousand Yosemites. Yet all these canyons unite to form one grand canyon, the most sublime spectacle on the earth. Pluck up Mt. Washington by the roots to the level of the sea and drop it headfirst into the Grand Canyon, and the dam will not force its waters over the walls. Pluck up the Blue Ridge and hurl it into the Grand Canyon, and it will not fill it."*—John Wesley Powell

come down to the river; but about eleven o'clock today we discover an Indian garden, at the foot of the wall on the right, just where a little stream, with a narrow flood-plain, comes down through a side canyon. Along the valley, the Indians have planted corn, using the water which burst out in springs at the foot of the cliff, for irrigation. The corn is looking quite well, but is not sufficiently advanced to give us roasting ears; but there are some nice, green squashes. We carry ten or a dozen of these on board our boats, and hurriedly leave, not willing to be. caught in the robbery, yet excusing ourselves by pleading our great want. We run down a short distance, to where we feel certain no Indians can follow; and what a kettle of squash sauce we make! True, we have no salt with which to season it, but it makes a fine addition to our unleavened bread and coffee. Never was fruit so sweet as these stolen squashes.

After dinner we push on again, making fine time, finding many rapids, but none so bad that we cannot run them with safety, and when we stop, just at dusk, and foot up our reckoning, we find we have run thirty-five miles again.

What a supper we make; unleavened bread, green squash sauce, and strong coffee. We have been for a few days on half rations, but we have no stint of roast squash.

A few days like this, and we are out of prison.

August 27.

This morning the river takes a more southerly direction. The dip of the rocks is to the north, and we are rapidly running into lower formations. Unless our course changes, we shall very soon run again into the granite. This gives us some anxiety. Now and then the river turns to the west, and excites hopes that are soon destroyed by another turn to the south. About nine o'clock we come to the dreaded rock. It is with no little misgiving that we see the river enter these black, hard walls. At its very entrance we have to make a portage; then we have to let down with lines past some ugly rocks. Then we run a mile or two farther, and then the rapids below can be seen.

About eleven o'clock we come to a place in the river where it seems much worse than any we have yet met in all its course. A little creek comes down from the left. We land first on the right, and clamber up over the granite pinnacles for a mile or two, but can see no way by which we can let down, and to run it would be sure destruction. After dinner we cross to examine it on the left.

High above the river we can walk along on the top of the granite, which is broken off at the edge, and set with crags and pinnacles, so that it is very difficult to get a view of the river at all. In my eagerness to reach a point where I can see the roaring fall below, I go too far on the wall, and can neither advance nor retreat. I stand with one foot on a little projecting rock, and cling with my hand fixed in a little crevice. Finding I am caught here, suspended 400 feet above the river, into which I should fall if my footing fails, I call for help. The men come, and pass me a line, but I cannot let go of the rock long enough to take hold of it. Then they bring two or three of the largest oars. All this takes time which seems very precious to me; but at last they arrive. The blade of one of the oars is pushed into a little crevice in the rock beyond me, in such a manner that they can hold me pressed against the wall. Then another is fixed in such a way that I can step on it, and thus I am extricated.

Still another hour is spent in examining the river from this side, but no good view of it is obtained, so now we return to the side that was first examined, and the afternoon is spent in clambering among the crags and pinnacles, and carefully scanning the river again. We find that the lateral streams have washed boulders into the river, so as to form a dam, over which the water makes a broken fall of eighteen or twenty feet; then there is a rapid, beset with rocks, for two or three hundred yards, while, on the other side, points of the wall project into the river. Then there is a second fall below; how great, we cannot tell. Then there is a rapid, filled with huge rocks, for one or two hundred yards. At the bottom of it, from the right wall, a great rock projects quite halfway across the river. It has a sloping surface extending up stream, and the water, coming down with all the momentum gained in the falls and rapids above, rolls up this inclined plane many feet, and tumbles over to the left. I decide that it is possible to let down over the first fall, then run near the right cliff to a point just above the second, where we can pull out into a little chute, and, having run over that in safety, we must pull with all our power across the stream, to avoid the great rock below. On my return to the boat, I announce to the men that we are to run it in the morning. Then we cross the river, and go into camp for the night on some rocks, in the mouth of the little side canyon.

After supper Captain Howland asks to have a talk with me. We walk up the little creek a short distance, and I soon find that his

Matcatameba Canyon.

object is to remonstrate against my determination to proceed. He thinks that we had better abandon the river here. Talking with him, I learn that his brother, William Dunn, and himself have determined to go no farther in the boats. So we return to camp. Nothing is said to the other men.

For the last two days, our course has not been plotted. I sit down and do this now, for the purpose of finding where we are by dead reckoning. It is a clear night, and I take out the sextant to make observations for latitude, and find that the astronomic determination agrees very nearly with that of the plot—quite as closely as might be expected, from a meridian observation on a planet. In a direct line, we must be about forty-five miles from the mouth of the Rio Virgen. If we can reach that point, we know that there are settlements up that river about twenty miles. This forty-five miles, in a direct line, will probably be eighty or ninety in the meandering line of the river. But then we know that there is comparatively open country for many miles above the mouth of the Virgen, which is our point of destination.

As soon as I determine all this, I spread my plot on the sand, and wake Howland, who is sleeping down by the river, and show him where I suppose we are, and where several Mormon settlements are situated.

We have another short talk about the morrow, and he lies down again; but for me there is no sleep. All night long, I pace up and down a little path, on a few yards of sand beach, along by the river. Is it wise to go on? I go to the boats again, to look at our rations. I feel satisfied that we can get over the danger immediately before us; what there may be below I know not. From our outlook yesterday, on the cliffs, the canyon seemed to make another great bend to the south, and this, from our experience heretofore, means more and higher granite walls. I am not sure that we can climb out of the canyon here, and, when at the top of the wall, I know enough of the country to be certain that it is a desert of rock and sand, between this and the nearest Mormon town, which, on the most direct line, must be seventy-five miles away. True, the late rains have been favorable to us, should we go out, for the probabilities are that we shall find water still standing in holes, and, at one time, I almost conclude to leave the river. But for years I have been contemplating the trip. To leave the exploration unfinished, to say that there is a

Catclaw bush just below Havasu Creek.

part of the canyon which I cannot explore, having already almost accomplished it, is more than I am willing to acknowledge, and I determine to go on.

I wake my brother, and tell him of Howland's determination, and he promises to stay with me; then I call up Hawkins, the cook, and he makes a like promise; then Sumner, and Bradley, and Hall, and they all agree to go on.

One of today's boats in the Granite Rapids.

August 28.

At last daylight comes, and we have breakfast, without a word being said about the future. The meal is solemn as a funeral. After breakfast, I ask the three men if they still think it best to leave us. The elder Howland thinks it is, and Dunn agrees with him. The younger Howland tries to persuade them to go on with the party, failing in which he decides to go with his brother.

Then we cross the river. The small boat is very much disabled, and unseaworthy. With the loss of hands, consequent on the departure of the three men, we shall not be able to run all the boats, so I decide to leave my *Emma Dean*.

Two rifles and a shot gun are given to the men who are going out. I ask them to help themselves to the rations, and take what they think to be a fair share. This they refuse to do, saying they have no fear but that they can get something to eat; but Billy, the cook, has a pan of biscuits prepared for dinner, and these he leaves on a rock.

Before starting, we take our barometers, fossils, the minerals, and some ammunition from the boat, and leave them on the rocks. We are going over this place as light as possible. The three men help us lift our boats over a rock twenty-five or thirty feet high, and let them down again over the first fall, and now we are all ready to start. The last thing before leaving, I write a letter to my wife, and give it to Howland. Sumner gives him his watch, directing that it be sent to his sister, should he not be heard from again. The records of the expedition have been kept in duplicate. One set of these is given to Howland, and now we are ready. For the last time, they entreat us not to go on, and tell us that it is madness to set out in this place; that we can never get safely through it; and, further, that the river turn again to the south into the granite, and a few miles of such rapids and falls will exhaust our entire stock of rations, and then it will be too late to climb out. Some tears are shed; it is rather

Travertine chute at Redrock Canyon.

a solemn parting; each party thinks the other is taking the dangerous course.

My old boat left, I go on board of the *Maid of the Canyon*. The three men climb a crag, that overhangs the river, to watch us off. The *Maid of the Canyon* pushes out. We glide rapidly along the foot of the wall, just grazing one great rock, then pull out a little into the chute of the second fall, and plunge over it. The open compartment is filled when we strike the first wave below, but we cut through it, and then the men pull with all their power toward the left wall, and swing clear of the dangerous rock below all right. We are scarcely a minute in running it, and find that, although it looked bad from above, we have passed many places that were worse.

The other boat follows without more difficulty. We land at the first practicable point below and fire our guns, as a signal to the men above that we have come over in safety. Here we remain a couple of hours, hoping that they will take the smaller boat and follow us. We are behind a curve in the canyon, and cannot see up to where we left them, and so we wait until their coming seems hopeless, and push on.*

And now we have a succession of rapids and falls until noon, all of which we run in safety. Just after dinner we come to another bad place. A little stream comes in from the left, and below there is a fall, and still below another fall. Above, the river tumbles down, over and among the rocks, in whirlpools and great waves, and the waters are lashed into mad, white foam. We run along the left, above this, and soon see that we cannot get down on this side, but it seems possible to let down on the other. We pull up stream again, for two or three hundred yards, and cross. Now there is a bed of basalt on this northern side of the canyon, with a bold escarpment, that seems to be a hundred feet high. We can climb it, and walk along its summit to a point where we are just at the head of the fall. Here the basalt is broken down again, so it seems to us, and I direct the men to take a line to the top of the cliff, and let the boats down along the wall. One man remains in the boat, to keep her clear of the rocks, and prevent her line from being caught on the projecting angles. I climb the cliff, and pass along to a point just over the fall, and descend by broken rocks, and find that the break of the fall is

Columnar basalt at Whitmore Wash.

---

* Today's canyoneers will find a simple bronze plaque on a wall above the now becalmed Separation Rapids (silted in by Lake Mead): "Seneca Howland, O. G. Howland, and William Dunn separated from the Original Powell Party, climbed to the North Rim, and were killed by the Indians."

above the break of the wall, so that we cannot land; and that still below the river is very bad, and that there is no possibility of a portage. Without waiting further to examine and determine what shall be done, I hasten back to the top of the cliff to stop the boats from coming down. When I arrive I find the men have let one of them down to the head of the fall. She is in swift water and they are not able to pull her back; nor are they able to go on with the line, as it is not long enough to reach the higher part of the cliff which is just before them; so they take a bight around a crag. I send two men back for the other line. The boat is in very swift water, and Bradley is standing in the open compartment, holding out his oar to prevent her from striking against the foot of the cliff. Now she shoots out into the stream and up as far as the line will permit, and then, wheeling, drives headlong against the rock, and then out and back again, now straining on the line, now striking against the rock. As soon as the second line is brought, we pass it down to him; but his attention is all taken up with his own situation, and he does not see that we are passing him the line. I stand on a projecting rock, waving my hat to gain his attention, for my voice is drowned by the roaring of the falls. Just at this moment I see him take his knife from the sheath and step forward to cut the line. He has evidently decided that it is better to go over with the boat as it is than to wait for her to be broken to pieces. As he leans over, the boat sheers again into the stream, the stem post breaks away and she is loose. With perfect composure Bradley seizes the great scull oar, places it in the stern rowlock, and pulls with all his power (and he is an athlete) to turn the bow of the boat down stream, for he wishes to go bow down, rather than to drift broadside on. One, two strokes he makes, and a third just as she goes over, and the boat is fairly turned, and she goes down almost beyond our sight, though we are more than a hundred feet above the river. Then she comes up again, on a great wave, and down and up, then around behind some great rocks, and is lost in the mad, white foam below. We stand frozen with fear, for we see no boat. Bradley is gone, so it seems. But now, away below, we see something coming out of the waves. It is evidently a boat. A moment more, and we see Bradley standing on deck, swinging his hat to show that he is all right. But he is in a whirlpool. We have the stem post of his boat attached to the line. How badly she may be disabled we know not. I direct Sumner and Powell to pass along the cliff, and see if they can reach him from below. Rhodes, Hall, and myself run to the other boat, jump aboard, push out, and away we go over the falls. A wave rolls over us, and our boat is unmanageable. Another great wave strikes us, the boat rolls over, and tumbles and tosses, I know not how. All I know is that Bradley is picking us up. We soon have all right again, and row to the cliff, and wait until Sumner and Powell can come. After a difficult climb they reach us. We run two or three miles farther, and turn again to the northwest, continuing until night, when we have run out of the granite once more.

August 29.

We start very early this morning. The river still continues swift, but we have no serious difficulty, and at twelve o'clock emerge from the Grand Canyon of the Colorado.

We are in a valley now, and low mountains are seen in the distance, coming to the river below. We recognize this as the Grand Wash.

A few years ago, a party of Mormons set out from St. George, Utah, taking with them a boat, and came down to the mouth of the Grand Wash, where they divided, a portion of the party crossing the river to explore the San Francisco Mountains. Three men—Hamblin, Miller, and Crosby—taking the boat, went on down the river to Callville, landing a few miles below the mouth of the Rio Virgen. We have their manuscript journal with us, and so the stream is comparatively well known.

Tonight we camp on the left bank, in a *mesquite* thicket.

The relief from danger, and the joy of success, are great. When he who has been chained by wounds to a hospital cot, until his canvas tent seems like a dungeon cell, until the groans of those who lie about, tortured with probe and knife, are piled up, a weight of horror on his ears that he cannot throw off, cannot forget, and until the stench of festering wounds and anesthetic drugs has filled the air with its loathsome burthen, at last goes into the open field, what a world he sees! How beautiful the sky; how bright the sunshine; what "floods of delirious music" pour from the throats of birds; how sweet the fragrance of earth, and tree, and blossom! The first hour of convalescent freedom seems rich recompense for all—pain, gloom, terror.

Something like this are the feelings we experience tonight. Ever before us has been an unknown danger, heavier than immediate peril. Every waking hour passed in the Grand Canyon has been one

A view downriver at Lower Granite Rapids.

Granite Falls, Kaibab Division, Grand Canyon.

Limestone chute at National Canyon.

*"Mountains of music swell in the rivers, hills of music billow in the creeks, and meadows of music murmur in the rills that ripple over the rocks, while other melodies are heard in the gorges of the lateral canyons. The Grand Canyon is a land of song."*

—John Wesley Powell

of toil. We have watched with deep solicitude the steady disappearance of our scant supply of rations, and from time to time have seen the river snatch a portion of the little left, while we were ahungered. And danger and toil were endured in those gloomy depths, where ofttimes the clouds hid the sky by day, and but a narrow zone of stars could be seen at night. Only during the few hours of deep sleep, consequent on hard labor, has the roar of the waters been hushed. Now the danger is over; now the toil has ceased; now the gloom has disappeared; now the firmament is bounded only by the horizon; and what a vast expanse of constellations can be seen!

The river rolls by us in silent majesty; the quiet of the camp is sweet; our joy is almost ecstasy. We sit till long after midnight, talking of the Grand Canyon, talking of home, but chiefly talking of the three men who left us. Are they wandering in those depths, unable to find a way out? are they searching over the desert lands above for water? are they nearing the settlements?

August 30.

We run through two or three short, low canyons today, and on emerging from one, we discover a band of Indians in the valley below. They see us, and scamper away in most eager haste, to hide among the rocks. Although we land, and call for them to return, not an Indian can be seen.

Two or three miles farther down, in turning a short bend in the river, we come upon another camp. So near are we before they can see us that I can shout to them, and being able to speak a little of their language, I tell them we are friends; but they all flee to the rocks, except a man, a woman, and two children. We land, and talk with them. They are without lodges, but have built little shelters of boughs, under which they wallow in the sand. The man is dressed in a hat; the woman in a string of beads only. At first they are evidently much terrified; but when I talk to them in their own language, and tell them we are friends, and inquire after people in the Mormon towns, they are soon reassured, and beg for tobacco. Of this precious article we have none to spare. Sumner looks around in the boat for something to give them, and finds a little piece of colored soap, which they receive as a valuable present, rather as a thing of beauty than as a useful commodity, however. They are either unwilling or unable to tell us anything about the Indians or white people, and so we push off, for we must lose no time.

We camp at noon under the right bank. And now, as we push out, we are in great expectancy, for we hope every minute to discover the mouth of the Rio Virgen.

Soon of the men exclaim: "Yonder's an Indian in the river." Looking for a few minutes, we certainly do see two or three persons. The men bend to their oars, and pull toward them. Approaching, we see that there are three white men and an Indian hauling a seine, and then we discover that it is just at the mouth of the long sought river.

As we come near, the men seem far less surprised to see us than we do to see them. They evidently know who we are, and, on talking with them, they tell us that we have been reported lost long ago, and that some weeks before, a messenger had been sent from Salt Lake City, with instructions for them to watch for any fragments or relics of our party that might drift down the stream.

Our new-found friends, Mr. Asa and his two sons, tell us that they are pioneers of a town that is to be built on the bank.

Eighteen or twenty miles up the valley of the Rio Virgen there are two Mormon towns, St. Joseph and St. Thomas. Tonight we dispatch an Indian to the last mentioned place, to bring any letters that may be there for us.

Our arrival here is very opportune. When we look over our store of supplies, we find about ten pounds of flour, fifteen pounds of dried apples, but seventy or eighty pounds of coffee.

Entrance to Paru'nuweap on the way to California.

August 31.

This afternoon the Indian returns with a letter, informing us that Bishop Leithhead, of St. Thomas, and two or three other Mormons are coming down with a wagon, bringing us supplies. They arrive about sundown. Mr. Asa treats us with great kindness, to the extent of his ability; but Bishop Leithhead brings in his wagon two or three dozen melons, and many other little luxuries, and we are comfortable once more.

September 1.

This morning Sumner, Bradley, Hawkins, and Hall, taking on a small supply of rations, start down the Colorado with the boats. It is their intention to go to Fort Mojave, and perhaps from there overland to Los Angeles.

Captain Powell, my brother, and myself return with Bishop Leithhead to St. Thomas. From St. Thomas we go to Salt Lake City.

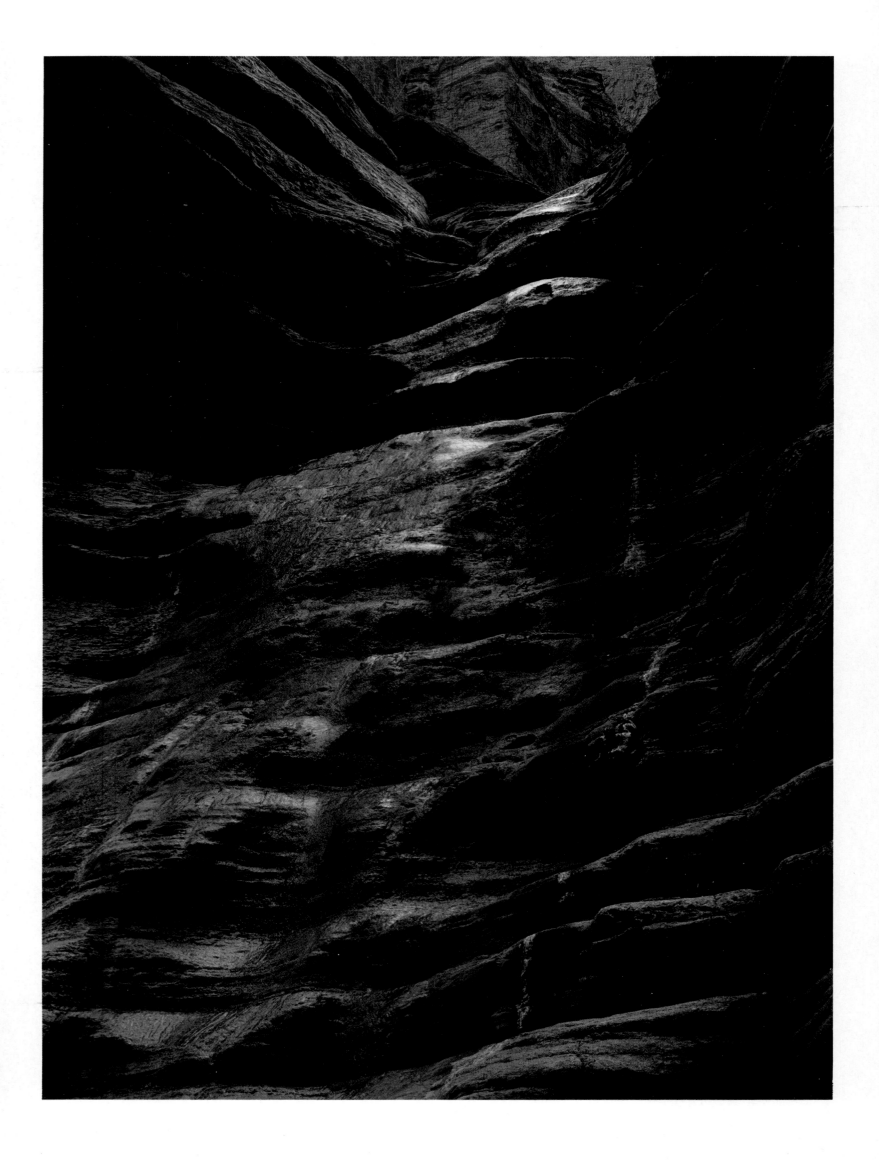

Eliot Porter
The Canyons of the
Colorado —
Past and Present
1969

Water seeping through Tuckup Canyon.

# Eliot Porter

## The Canyons of the
## Colorado –
## Past and Present
## 1969

Lake Powell commemorates Glen Canyon in much the same sense that a statue commemorates a famous man. But sculptured marble can no more give satisfaction to those who know a living man's charms than can the lake that fills Glen Canyon replace the beauties it has submerged in the memories of those who journeyed on the river that flowed until 1963.

A monument to a person is thus an inadequate reminder to his close friends; it speaks only to the public in historical terms. It celebrates his public life; his gentler private qualities and personal attachments are not communicated. And so with Glen Canyon, Lake Powell celebrates the short history of the construction of the dam that destroyed it; of the filling of the basin behind the dam with water of the Colorado River; of the development of commercial facilities on the shores of the lake; and of the ever-increasing crowds that come with high-speed motorboats and water skis to make use of these facilities. These are what Lake Powell memorializes. But the long unrecorded secret history of Glen Canyon, fragments of which survive fleetingly in the minds of the canyon's few explorers, lies drowned and lost.

To the motorboatist the lake presents superb opportunities for racing about in his high-powered craft. He can speed for hundreds of miles from gasoline pump to gasoline pump with hardly more than a glance at the half-submerged tapestried sandstone walls. When boredom overtakes him he can break the monotony with water skiing, an activity that too soon palls. Always seeking new artificial thrills to lessen the drag of time, he roars into narrow, flooded tributary canyons, side-slipping around the tight S-curves at thirty miles an hour.

Not long ago one could walk in these side canyons beside reflecting pools upon a smoothed-out sandstone floor in an atmosphere aglow with filtered sun and sky. The boatman, to whom the undammed river could once have provided wondrous experiences, knows nothing of these lost glories, regrets them not, and belittles them in his ignorance. Nowhere in the world are these drowned canyons duplicated. In place of infinite variety, awesome convolutions, mysterious and secret recesses, glowing painted walls and golden streams, we have received in exchange a featureless sheet of water, a dead basin into which all the flotsam from the surrounding land accumulates with no place to go: a sink for sediments and the trash carelessly scattered about by throngs of visitors. The exchange is one of the greatest frauds ever perpetrated by responsible government on an unsuspecting people. They have been cheated out of a birthright without ever knowing they possessed it.

The fern-bedecked amphitheaters, where the only sounds heard were the plink of dripping water or the sudden cascading song of a canyon wren, the mirroring pools under a curving, banded cliff, and the sheets of silent sliding water are no more. The ends of the side canyons are now clogged with driftwood and the debris from suffocated and dying trees. The banks are everywhere undermined and are slipping into the lake, leaving behind unstable sandy walls of exposed roots. Mud that formerly was flushed down into the big river by freshets and flash floods is deposited now in the shallows, covering the approaches to the upper reaches of the canyons with quaking layers of ooze and quicksand. In these backwaters loaded with decay and decomposition an explosion of algal growth is taking place, turning the water into a murky green soup and coating it with thick layers of scum. Scattered throughout the packed wreckage of vegetation are Coke and beer cans, plastic containers, film cartons, packaged food wrappings, and empty suntan lotion bottles, the discard of an irresponsible civilization.

A dead lake has replaced a living river, and even the dead lake is threatened with further deterioration from pollution. Where recently flowing water lapped at green banks; where willows, tamarisk, cottonwood, and oak groves crowded to the water's edge; where teaming riparian life filled all the niches in the ribboned oasis carved by the river into the Colorado Desert; where great blue herons waded and fished through the summer months; where beaver burrowed into the

Side view of the lower section of Travertine Falls.

150

clay banks; where lizards darted among the rocks of the talus slopes; where deer came down from the dry highlands to drink and browse; and where in spring a dozen kinds of warblers sang or built their nests in the budding thickets—now barren rock is all that remains. Life is gone, drowned, dispersed, departed, extinguished for want of room and a place to breed. The plunging cliffs are licked by the wake of passing boats reflected from wall to wall. No songs of birds now are heard; in their stead we have the whine and roar of internal combustion engines.

This is the monument men have built—you and I—not to the lost Eden so few knew, but to their engineering ingenuity and ruthless ability to transform the land, to remake it simply for the sake of re-making it, thoughtlessly, improvidently. Gone is indeed an Eden, an Eden of multifarious, wondrous canyons, some deep, dark, and narrow, some wide and long, some cut in bare rock and boulder-strewn, some green and sunlit. They all bore names suited to their particular attributes: Mystery, Twilight, Dungeon, Labyrinth, Cathedral, Hidden Passage. And one, because of difficult access, was called Lost Eden—a name that now speaks the fate of Glen Canyon.

A few miles below Glen Canyon Dam, at Lee's Ferry, the Grand Canyon of the Colorado begins. If the plans of the engineers had prevailed, long stretches of this incomparable geological phenomenon would suffer the same fate as Glen Canyon. Fortunately, owing to the dedicated efforts of those who appreciate the aesthetic and scientific value of this famous gorge more than the commercial uses to which it could be put for the profit of an unenlightened few, these schemes have finally been forestalled.

Before the construction of Glen Canyon Dam, Lee's Ferry was the only available crossing of the Colorado River between Hite, at the mouth of White Canyon more than one hundred miles to the north, and Hoover Dam, over three hundred miles downstream. Nor does a road crossing exist where the Grand Canyon comes to an end as the river debouches from lower Granite Gorge at Grand Wash cliffs near the head of Lake Mead. At Lee's Ferry boat trips through Grand Canyon start. Here the river, flowing due south through Marble Gorge, at the beginning of its penetration of the Kaibab Plateau, has ground its way down through hundreds of feet of layered limestone. These hard gray metamorphosed rocks, polished by the fast-flowing, sediment-laden water, give the gorge its name. Below its confluence at mile 62 with the Little Colorado, the river swings with seeming perversity in a long arc westward into the heart of the plateau.

The apparent paradox of a river flowing into and bisecting a mountain instead of being deflected from its course becomes understandable in terms of the tectonic forces involved in the extensive upwarping of the entire Colorado Plateau. The Grand Canyon by geological measure is young, perhaps no older than a few million years. The first canyon geologists pictured the Colorado River during early Miocene times as flowing through lowlands on much the same route it takes today. Eventually the land began to rise but the river maintained its course by eroding its channel deeper to keep pace with the uplift. During the several millions of years since the upheaval began, the Mesozoic strata were swept away from the rising land exposing the Paleozoic layers. The Colorado gouged into these formations layer by layer until it cut through the great unconformities of the Cambrian and Precambrian Eras. Below the Precambrian sediments the billion-year-old record of earth history dims into uncertainty. The rocks dating from that time have been transformed by pressure and temperature and igneous intrusion into crystalline schists and granites. Though they are dark and hard, the river has ground into them hundreds of feet. Today the river still cuts and the uplift apparently continues.

On the basis of recent geological studies, it is now believed that the Kaibab upwarp, which was first supposed to have occurred in the Miocene, in fact began many millions of years earlier. The effect of the uplift was to create a divided river system in which the upper Colorado Plateau drained to the southeast into the Gulf of Mexico or into Lake Bidahochi in eastern Arizona. The lower part of the plateau west of the Kaibab drained away through the Hualapai system to the southwest. It is postulated that the western system captured the upper Colorado drainage by headward extension into the Kaibab Plateau until it coalesced with tributaries of the latter to establish a single through-flowing river. Although much evidence has been gathered to support this view, the final stage is difficult to reconcile with the present physiography of the canyon.

Grand Canyon is as different from Glen Canyon as night is from day. Grand Canyon represents the climax of the river's grinding effort to maintain its course; and young as Grand Canyon is, the river has been here longer at its enforced labor than in Glen Canyon. More cubic miles of rock have been pulverized to sand and washed away in the gorge that splits the Kaibab uplift than in most known river canyons, and the task was accomplished in shorter time than a similar task by any comparable major river. The erosion of Glen Canyon is a still more recent product of the Colorado River. Its creation has consumed scarcely a tenth the time that has elapsed in the formation of Grand Canyon.

Historians measure time in terms of human lives—in generations and hundreds of years. Geologists, historians of the earth, think of events in cycles that span vastly greater periods—thousands and millions of years. But even a million years is only one hundredth of one per cent of the known age of the earth. The Colorado River probably began its carving of Glen Canyon not more than one million years ago, that is, in the Quarternary Period, the last two tenths of the Cenozoic Era—the Age of Mammals—when man's anthropoid ancestors were beginning their first tentative experiments with an erect posture and the crudest tools.

To appreciate the evanescence of topography under the working of erosive forces it is necessary to consider change in the perspective of geological time. The Colorado River and its tributaries have sliced into the Mesozoic sandstones of what is now southern Utah to a depth of about a thousand feet. Assuming that this process began a million years ago, the annual abrasion, if continued at a constant rate, would have been a little over one hundredth of an inch a year, an amount unnoticeable even when totaled over a human lifetime. At double this rate the cutting still would have been inappreciable, but we can guess that for a time at the beginning of this period, and intermittently since then, the river eroded its channel very much more rapidly. Had the channeling been a slow drawn-out affair, we would not find today the abrupt profiles of the tortuous, highly convoluted tributary canyons or the vertical cliffs bordering the main river. They would show the gradual slopes of more mature canyons. The precipitous walls would have been broken down and the narrow slots in the sandstone with overhanging sides would have been opened up and widened at the top. We know that the rate of erosion in very recent times, within the last few thousand years at most, has not been a continuous steady process. It has fluctuated greatly, in conjunction probably with climatic changes. The evidence for this sequence of events is clear to read in the deposits of sand dozens of feet thick found in many of the side canyons. Not so long ago the rounded, bare rock bottoms of these tributaries were exposed. Thundering turbulent streams, the runoff from the land above of constant heavy rains, undercut the sides and hollowed out the bends. Water racing down the narrow channels to join the main river carried all before it in a grinding flood.

As the climate changed and the rains diminished, the floods in Glen Canyon became less frequent and less violent. Then the streams began to deposit their sediments, to build up layer on layer of mud and sand over the rock floors. The seeds of trees and grass and all manner of plants germinated in the deposits within protected alcoves. The vegetation grew and spread, covering the banks, and the streams became gentle brooks flowing meandering courses among the reeds and horsetails and willows. The period of fast erosion had come to an end with the development of a drier climate. The canyons had become spring-fed green oases in a desert land. However, nothing in nature—nothing in life or land or climate—long remains unchanged, change being the order of things. Within the recent past the tributaries to Glen Canyon began to reverse the process of sedimentation; deposits were cut down and washed out, leaving isolated and dying groves of trees high above the streams that formerly kept them alive. Steep eroded banks of sand developed, out of which masses of exposed roots dangled. And the old curved rock floors of some of the narrowest canyons were again exposed. Perhaps a new period of fast cutting was on the way. If this were the case, the trend has been interrupted by the imposition of Glen Canyon Dam across the channel of flow. The dam is a temporary block to a course of events about which geologists have only just begun to speculate. But in the vastness of geological time we know that the episode of the dam is but the blink of an eye.

Grand Canyon reflects less dramatically the same climatic oscillations that accompanied the Pleistocene glaciations, which played such an important role in the shaping of Glen Canyon. With the river taking ten times more time to gouge out Grand Canyon, the results of the changing weather—where evident at all—are visible as secondary alterations of its towering sides and not in the adamantine rocks of the dark gorge where the Colorado River was flowing while Glen Canyon was still in its infancy. The different manifestations of the wet period are attributable both to the relative ages of the canyons and to the formations through which they have been eroded. Glen Canyon was cut into the softer Navajo and Wingate sandstones and shales of the Mesozoic Era. The later formations, which covered these enormously

thick layers of Aeolian origin of the reptile age, have been completely swept away over vast areas. Only scanty evidence of earlier canyons in the vanished Cenozoic strata exists today.

The formations now exposed, out of which the ancient river has hewn the multicolored buttes and temples and soaring cliffs of the present-day Grand Canyon, belong to the periods of the Paleozoic from the Permian to the Cambrian. Many unconformities are found between the strata of these periods that tell of great mountain ranges upthrust and totally washed away. What survived in great part is metamorphosed limestone produced from the calcareous remains of marine animals that sifted down through the waters of shallow seas for years beyond reckoning to build deposits of immense thickness. These limestones compose the walls of Marble Canyon and the Red Wall limestone cliffs high on the sides of Grand Canyon proper. They are stained by the traces of iron in washings from layers above of more complex composition, but where they plunge into the river in Marble Canyon or where angular talus fragments are exposed to the action of sediment-loaded running water the rock is highly polished. It is from these multifaceted, glistening surfaces that Marble Gorge derives its name.

Harder than Navajo sandstone though limestone is, and less readily abraded, it is more quickly eroded by solvent action. Water flowing into cracks and fractures, especially if weakly acid, dissolves the stone, enlarging the channel and creating in time aquifers of great extent and complexity. Limestone country is famous for its caverns and underground rivers produced in this way. In Marble Canyon these channels have in places near the water's edge coalesced into a honeycomb of cavities. In Grand Canyon, aquifers in the Red Wall limestone feed springs on the canyon sides where the lime-laden waters, on exposure to air, redeposit the dissolved mineral in formations like those that surround hot springs or that occur as stalactites and stalagmites in caves. These accretions, which in time build up into huge mounds of reticulated porous stone called travertine, are found in many places on the lower walls of Grand Canyon. The great majority today are dried up and inactive, but a few of the springs, notably Travertine Grotto, Travertine Falls, and the warm springs below Lava Falls, still flow.

During periods of much greater precipitation in the Southwest, associated with the farthest advance of the continental ice sheet, when the tributaries of Glen Canyon were roaring torrents, the travertine springs of Grand Canyon were all active and overflowing. Then the canyon

Mimulus and moss, Travertine Falls.

walls were greener than today. As with the few that still run, all then were surrounded with thickets of canes and willows, and the terraced limey basins were bordered with wild celery and water cress. Hundreds of waterfalls poured from the cliffs of the inner gorge or shot down inclined chutes built of reprecipitated lime and plunged into space. From the evidence of the disintegrating and discolored travertine hanging on the precipices like candle drippings, one can easily imagine the beautiful and awesome spectacle that Grand Canyon presented in the late Pleistocene. Not only were the canyon walls alive with inflowing water and luxuriant vegetation, the river itself was many times greater than today. It filled its channel from wall to wall. It was an irresistible torrent of hundreds of thousands of cubic feet of water, thick with rock dust and debris, passing by each second, which could roll house-sized boulders before it with ease.

When one contemplates this re-created Colorado of scarcely 50,000 years ago, the river of Grand Canyon today even at its greatest flood seems tame indeed. But in our time it has been tamed still more by the building of Glen Canyon Dam. Its water carries no burden of silt from the mountains of Wyoming or Colorado, or from the deserts of Utah. The upper Colorado River, the Dirty Devil, the Escalante, the San Juan, and all the smaller creeks drop their sediments now in the still waters of Lake Powell. Below the dam, except when the Paria is in flood, the river run clear and blue-green as far as its junction with the Little Colorado. The rapids in Marble Gorge are foaming white. And on those infrequent occasions when the Little Colorado—usually a thick brown soup—runs milky blue like Havasu Creek, the main river may be siltless all the way to Lake Mead.

For nearly a century the Grand Canyon has been known from its rim. The magnificence of the view from the topmost sharp-edged cliff down into the terraced interior is world famous. The awesome ambiguity of scale fascinates or repels those who gaze into the canyon for the first time. The torn inverted landscape lying spread out below is a raw wound in the earth's skin in which the exposed anatomy has the colors of torn flesh. One looks down on buttes, the size of many an eastern mountain. that rise from plains thousands of feet below, though they appear to be almost within arm's reach. Distances to far cliffs and towers that fade into the indistinct purple haze are measureless. The river, glimpsed in places, seems to be directly below one's feet. So tiny it appears, no bigger than a mountain brook, that the first reaction is

Hidden passage, Glen Canyon. Scenes like this are memories.

incredulity: Can this stream indeed have carved the whole vast landscape? That it is indeed the architect becomes more convincing as one descends into Granite Gorge and begins to hear and see the river's power.

Much less known is Grand Canyon from its river level. Millions have seen it from the top, whereas until the last few years hundreds only had journeyed through its inner gorge. Recently these numbers have increased many-fold, until today they have reached into the thousands, but are still far short of the numbers of those who have merely looked down.

When Powell first explored the Colorado in 1869 it was an unknown river, considered unnavigable by most western explorers, and the Indians too warned that any attempt to float down it would end in certain death. No one knew how many or how great the cataracts were, or whether an impassable fall might be encountered at a place where no return was possible. No wonder then, after months of travel, half starved and exhausted, that Powell's men were depressed and discouraged by their first sight of the Granite Gorge. After the calm peace of Glen Canyon and to a lesser degree Marble, they could not view its black cliffs as less than portents of disaster. To them the gorge presented no relieving aspects; the narrowing walls were gloomy, oppressive, and foreboding. The adventure to them was worn thin. They could think of nothing but the end of the journey and escape.

Today, now that the river has been mapped and charted, a boat trip through Grand Canyon offers few of these frightening aspects. The rapids are all known, named, and measured, and the difficulties they present to navigation have been assessed. They all have been run by boats and rubber rafts; few are ever portaged or lined. Cataracts are encountered by today's boatmen with less trepidation than may have affected Powell. But there is still plenty of excitement in the old river. Each rapid is a separate adventure, each has its special thrill. All share in common, however, the excitement provided by the swift glide down the smooth tongue where the river drops off at the head of the rapid and funnels with increasing speed into the first waves, and then by the crash of water over the boat. It is a thrill that never diminishes and which draws people back to the Grand Canyon time and again. Another dimension, recently added to river experience, which would have been considered suicide when Norman Nevills was leading his cataract-boat trips thirty years ago, but was found by the more enthusiastic white-water adventurers to be quite safe, is to float through some of the worst rapids in a life jacket. The swimmer bobs along over the standing waves with little sense of motion until he glances at the bank, when he discovers to his surprise how fast he moves.

Regardless of modern innovations that have increased the safety of river running, one's life during a trip through Grand Canyon is dominated by the river. The river determines almost every detail of daily routine. Because its flow fluctuates on a diurnal rhythm, controlled by the release of water through the penstocks of Glen Canyon Dam, this domination is more true today than it was before the construction of the dam. The river decides where one camps, how far one can travel in a day, at what time one can most easily navigate a rapid, and how it should be done.

Cataracts occur on the average of one every mile or two throughout the whole three hundred miles of Grand Canyon. They vary greatly in roughness and gradient, from a drop of a few feet spread over a quarter of a mile to more than fifteen feet in a hundred yards. Nevertheless, there are quiet stretches of water, of which Conquistador Aisle is one of the longest. In these one drifts along at a leisurely pace beside the black-veined walls of polished schist in sunless chasms which, having ceased to arouse a sense of foreboding, provide welcome relief from the heat of the midsummer sun. In the lower-gorge walls of crumbling lava, that came tumbling into the canyon during an ancient period of volcanism, are masses of sliced-off hexagonal columns, some of which are stacked vertically as though to buttress the cliff, others projecting end out, horizontally, like immense black honeycombs. No longer do these old lava flows carry the ominous implications they correctly bore for Powell, who in this part of the canyon came upon the two greatest rapids of the Colorado River, excepting the falls at Glenwood Springs—Lava Falls and Lava Cliff—the latter now submerged by the headwaters of Lake Mead.

Never is the canyon traveler out of hearing of the sounds of the river. Its voice, heard from the smooth reaches between rapids, is muffled by distance, yet it forms part of the background of noise that scarcely rises above the faint concoction of sounds made by the murmuring wind and lapping ripples. But more persistent than these, as one glides toward its origin, the voice swells to a loud rumble that dominates all other sounds until, as the foaming cataract comes into sight, they are overwhelmed by the deafening crash of water. It is the roar of a dozen

freight trains crossing a trestle. The thunder of the river is its basic, authentic endowment. It accompanies one throughout the day and lulls one to sleep at night. But it can be ignored, pushed aside into some recess of consciousness and forgotten, until at the end of the trip as the boats float out onto still water, and the roar of the river fades back in space and time, all at once it is missed and one recognizes that the basic state of silence has returned. This is a regretful moment when one wishes he could be transferred back again into the turmoil and activity of the canyon.

Today's scene in the flooded canyons.

*Emerging from the underground passage, the ghostly traveler comes*
*to a great fissure or chasm called the* Pa'-kūp. *This must be crossed*
*to reach the beautiful valley. Spanning the chasm there is a narrow*
*bridge called* Na-gum'-pa-sūg. *None but the brave dare cross this bridge;*
*this is the last but most fearful trial to the ghostly traveler. On the*
*other side of the chasm stand the daughters of* Shin-au'-av *who beckon*
*to and encourage the poor frightened ghost to attempt this last great*
*danger. If his courage stands the test they greet his arrival with many*
*and excessive demonstrations of joy.*

*—Southern Paiute legend*

*They came to the Colorado River and Spider-Woman said (to Ti-yo),*
*"You are near your father's house; now I leave you. You are now the*
*chief of the Antelopes. Through you shall come rain, and snow, and*
*green grass. From you shall the songs proceed; to you shall the songs*
*return; but nothing, no reward or benefit, to you, or to me, nothing*
*shall come."*

*—Hopi legend*

# Index

(Figures in italics indicate illustrations)

Alarcón, Hernando de, 15
American Fur Company, 14
American fur trade, 17–18
Anasazi Pueblo peoples, 14, 15
Arizona, 118
Armijo, Antonio, 17
Asa, Mr., 145
Ashley, General William, 14, 40, 48, 49
Ashley Falls, 40
Ashley's Creek, 49

Badlands, *32*
Baker, James, 40
Baker, John, 36
Beaman, E. O., 11, 21, 55 n.
Billy the cook, 139
"Bishop, The," wife of *Tsau'-wi-at,* 62
Black Canyon, 16, 20
Black's Fork, 33
Book Cliffs, 17
Bow-knot, 74
Bradley, G. Y., 29–30, 34, 50, 53–55, 57, 58 n., 70, 77, 78, 82, 83, 110 n., 139, 141, 145
Bright Angel River, 117–118
Brown's Park, 41
Buck Farm Canyon, *61*
Bureau of American Ethnology, 11
Bureau of Ethnology, 11
Butte of the Cross, 75

California, Gulf of, 15
Canyon Country of the Colorado River, 9, 18, 107–145, 147–165; map, *26.* See also individual topographical entries
Canyons, flooded, *162*
Cárdenas, García López de, discovers Grand Canyon, 15–16
Cataract Canyon, 15, 18, 82, 91, 99
Cathedral Canyon, 152
Callville, 14, 142
Colorado Chiquito (Little Colorado), 104, 106, 107, 128, 131. See also Colorado River; Grand River
Colorado Desert, 150
Colorado Plateau, 16, 153
Colorado River (Grand River), 14, 16, 20, 27, 78, 79–107, 147–165; Powell's first trip through (map), *26.* See also Canyon Country of the Colorado River; Colorado Chiquito; Grand River; Little Colorado River
Conquistador Aisle, 161
Coronado, Francisco Vásquez de, 15, 16
Cortes, Sea of (Gulf of California), 15
Crosby, 142

Crossing of the Fathers, 16–17, 97

Davis Gulch, on Escalante River, *30*
Deer Creek, *112, 114, 119*
Dellenbaugh, Frederick S., 89; account of second (1871) expedition, 107
Desolation Canyon, *67,* 70
Dirty Devil River, 91, 158
Disaster Falls, wreck at, *48*
Dodds, Captain, 62
Dolores River, 16
Domínguez, Francisco Atanasio, discovers Green River, 16
Duchesne River, 14
Dungeon Canyon, 152
Dunn, William, 9, 20, 29, 48, 49, 67, 69, 91, 137, 139, 140 n., 141
Dutton, Clarence, 11

Echo Park, to mouth of Uinta River, 53–63
Echo Rock, 53
Elves Cavern, *122;* waterfall in, *127*
Escalante, Father Francisco Silvestre Vélez de, explorations of, 16–17, 97
Escalante River, 21, 158; Davis Gulch on the, *30*
*Explorations of the Colorado River of the West and Its Tributaries* (Powell), 21
Explorer's Canyon, at Lake Powell, *22*

Fennemore, James, 11
Flaming Gorge, 27–36, *34;* to Gate of Lodore, 36–42
Fluted schist, *81*
Fort Mojave, 20, 145
Frémont, John C., 18, 20, 41
Fremont peoples, 15

Gable with pinnacles, *117*
Garcés, Francisco Hermenegildo, 16
Geographical and Geological Survey of the Rocky Mountain Region, 9
Geological Survey, 23
Gila River, 15
Gilbert, G. K., 11
Glen Canyon, 14, 23, *94,* 97, 149, 153–155, 157, *159,* 160
Glen Canyon Dam, 152, 158, 161
Glenwood Springs, 161
Goodman, Frank, 29, 31, 45–47, 63
Grand Canyon of the Colorado, 9, 12, *76, 78, 90,* 107–145; early exploration of, 15–17; first white men to see, 15;

Grand Canyon *(Cont.)*
geological age of, 153; head of the, *110;* looking east, *110;* looking east at Torowep, Arizona, *111;* photographed, 11; Stony Creek, *90, 95;* Tapeats Creek emptying into, *103, 105.* See also Canyon Country of the Colorado River; Colorado Chiquito; Colorado River
Grand (Colorado) River, 9, 15, 20, 27, 78, 97: from junction of Green and, to Little Colorado, 77–107; from mouth of Uinta River to junction of Green River and, 63–75; junction of Green River and, *75,* 79-80. See also Colorado River
Grand Wash, 142, 152
Granite dykes and schist, *98*
Granite Falls, Kiabab Division, Grand Canyon, *142;* upstream, *3*
Granite Gorge, 152, 160
Granite Rapids, *84–85, 139;* running the, 107, *108–109*
Gray Canyon, *71*
Great Basin, 18
Great Salt Lake, 17
"Great Surveys," 9
Green River, 9, 11, 14, 15, 17, 18, 20, 21, 78, 97; at Canyon of Lodore, *49;* at confluence with Colorado River, 27; discovery of, 16; junction of Grand and, to Little Colorado, 77–107; from mouth of Uinta River to junction of Grand River and, 63–75; second expedition on, *42;* start of Powell's trip on, *27;* a valley of, *31;* and Yampa River, 52–56
Green River badlands, *32*
Green River City, 27, *121;* to Flaming Gorge, 27–36
Green River country, 12
Green River Station, 9, 14
Gunnison, Captain J. W., 18, 72
Gunnison Butte, *71*
Gunnison River, 16
Gypsum Canyon, 87

Hall, Andrew, 29, 31, 66, 83, 139, 141, 145
Hamblin, Jacob, 20, 142
Hattan, Andy, 55 n.
Havasu Creek, *136,* 158
Havasupai Canyon, 16
Hawikuh, 15, 16
Hawkins, W. R., 29, 31, 139, 145
Hayden, F. V., 9
"Hell's Half Mile" (Canyon of Lodore), *44,* 49

Henry Mountains, 11, 21, *96*
Henry's Fork, 33, 34
Hidden Passage, Glen Canyon, *35*
Hidden Passage Canyon, 152
Hillers, John K. (Jack), 11, 21, 34 n., 55 n., *60*
Hite, 152
Hogbacks, *41*
Hoover Dam, 20, 152
Horseshoe Canyon, 37
House Rock Canyon, *43*
House Rock Rapids, sculptured rock at, *38*
Howland brothers, O. F. and Seneca, 9, 20, 29, 31, 45, 47, 55, 67, 69, 83, 135, 137, 139, 140 n.
Humboldt, Alexander von, maps of, 17

Illinois State Natural History Society, 12
Illinois State Normal University, 12
Illinois Wesleyan University, Powell as Professor of Geology at, 12
Indians: Apache, 15; Cohonina, 14; Gosiute, 17; Havasupai, 14; Hopi, 14, 15; Navajo, 15, 97; Paiute, 17; "Shinumo," 15; Shivwits Paiute, 9; Shoshone, 17; southern Paiute, 15, 17; southern Ute, 16; "Tabuats" Utes, 11; Uinta, 60, 61, *62;* Ute, 15, 16, 67; Zuni, 15
Inner Gorge, *73, 113*
Ives, Lieutenant Joseph Christmas, 18

Johnson, hunter and Indian trader, 63, 66
Jones, S. V., 55 n., 79 n.
Julien, Denis, 18

Kaibab Division, *142*
Kaibab Plateau, 142, 153, 154
Kanab, Utah, founded, 20
Kanab Canyon, *124*
Kanab Creek, 11; grapevines in, *129*
King, Clarence, 9
Kingfisher Canyon, 37
Kino, Fray Eusebio, explores Colorado River, 16
"Kivas," 92, 93

Labyrinth Canyon, 18, 74, 92, 152
Lake Mead, 140 n., 152, 158, 161
Lake Powell, 23, 149–152, 158, 165; Explorer's Canyon at, *22*
Land of Standing Rocks, 74
Lava Canyon, *68, 130*

Lava Cliff, 161
Lava Falls, *130*, 157, 161
Lee, John D., 20
Lee's Ferry (Lonely Dell), 11, 16, 152
Leithhead, Bishop, 145
Little Colorado, 104, 106, 107, 153, 158; from junction of Grand and Green rivers to mouth of, 77–107; mouth of the, *113. See also* Colorado Chiquito
Lodore, Canyon of, 42–52, *44, 45*; Green River at, *49*
Lodore, Gate of, from Flaming Gorge to, 36–42
Lonely Dell (Lee's Ferry), 11, 20
Long's Peak, 53; Powell's ascent of, 12
Lost Eden Canyon, 152
Lower Granite Rapids, *142*

Macomb, Captain John M., 20
Marble Canyon, *46, 61*, 102, 104, *106*, 123, 157, 160; Vasey's Paradise near, *51*
Marble Gorge, 152, 158; rapid in, *54;* side canyon near, *64–65*
Matcatameba Canyon, *76, 135*
Mexican War, 18
Mexico, 118
Miera y Pacheco, Bernardo de, cartographer, 17, 18
Mille Crag Bend, 91
Miller, 142
Moab, Utah, 17
Monterey, Mission of, 97
Mormons, 49, 97, 99, 120, 137, 142, 144, 145
Mount Dawes, 55
Mount Hawkins, 57
Mountain Meadows Massacre, 20
"Mountain Men," 18
Music Temple, 96
Mystery Canyon, 152

Narrow Canyon, 91, 92
National Canyon, Limestone Chute at, *143*
Nevills, Norman, 160
New Mexico, 15, 118
Newberry, Dr. John Strong, 20

Oak Glens, 97
Old Spanish Trail, 17

"On the Physical Features of the Valley of the Colorado" (Powell), 21
Oraiby, 118

Paria Creek, 99, 158
Paru'nuweap, *145*
Pattie, James Ohio, 18
Petroglyphs, 15
Plateaus, high, *31*
*Political Essay on the Kingdom of New Spain* (Humboldt), 17
Porter, Eliot, "The Canyons of the Colorado—Past and Present," 147–165
Powell, Emma, née Dean, wed to John Wesley Powell, 12
Powell, John Wesley, 161; articles on Canyon Country, 21; background and early life, 11–12; becomes director of United States Geological Survey, 9, 11; death of, 23; "Diary of First Trip through Grand Canyon," 25–145; directs Bureau of American Ethnology, 11; during Civil War, 12; explores Green River Country, 12; first exploration of Colorado, 160; and Hamblin, 20; and Indians of Canyon country, 11; letter on Grand Canyon country, 12; loss of arm, 9, 12; rescue of, 53–55, *53;* retires, 23; second expedition, *33, 89;* second expedition members, *42;* with second river party, *27;* studies of Canyon Country, 21, 23; traverses Grand Canyon, 9, 25–145; weds Emma Dean, 12
Powell, W., 29, 70, 79, 80, 82, 83, 101, 104, 141, 142, 145
Preuss, Charles, 18
Pueblos, 118

Rainbow Park, 58
Red Wall, 157
Red Wall Cavern, *59;* alcove in, *125*
Redbud Canyon, on San Juan River, *18*
Redrock Canyon, *138;* granite-schist formations near, *132–133*

*Report on the Lands of the Arid Region of the United States* (Powell), 23
Rhodes, 141
Rio Grande, 15
Rio Virgen, 137. *See also* Virgin River
River rapids, *11*
Rivera, Don Juan María de, explores tributaries of Colorado River, 16
Rocky Mountains, 55, 58
Roubidoux, Antoine, 18
Running a rapid, *80*

St. George, Utah, 16, 142
St. Joseph, 145
St. Thomas, 145
Salt Lake City, 20, 49, 145
San Francisco Mountains, 142
San Gabriel, California, 17
San Juan River, 14, 16, 94, 96, 158; Redbud Canyon on, *18*
San Rafael River, 72
Santa Fé, 16, 17, 18
*Scribners' Monthly*, Powell's articles in, 21
Separation Rapids, 9, 140 n.
Seven-Mile Canyon, pool at, *28*
Sevier Lake, 17
Sevier Valley, 17
Side Canyon, *57*
Sierra La Sal Mountains, 75, 79, 96
Smith, Jedediah, 18
Spanish Trail, 18
Split Mountain Canyon, 58
Stillwater Canyon, 18, 75
Stoney Creek, *90;* in Grand Canyon, 95
Sumner, J. C., 29, 47, 48, 66, 67, 77, 139, 141, 142, 145
Surprise Valley, side canyon, *121*
Swallow Canyon, 41
Sweetwater Mountains, 55

Tamarisks, above granite rapids, *84–85*
Tapeats Creek, *103, 105*
Taylor, Bayard, travels in Colorado, 29
Thompson, 79 n.
Thunder River Falls, *105*
*Toom'-pin wu-near' Tu-weap'*, 78-79
Torowep, Arizona, *111*
Továr, Captain Pedro de, discovers Grand Canyon, 15–16

Tower Park, 74
Travertine Falls, *151, 156, 157*
Travertine Grotto, 157
Triplet Falls, 49
Tuckup Canyon, *146*
Tusayan, Province of, 118
Tusayan people, 92
25-Mile Canyon, 47
Twilight Canyon, 152

Uinkarets Plateau, 20
Uinta Agency, 62
Uinta Basin, 14, 18, 21
Uinta Mountains, 11, 32, 33, 55, 58
Uinta River, 62; from Echo Park to mouth of, 52–63; from mouth of, to junction of Grand and Green rivers, 63–75
Uncompahgre River, 16
United States Army, explores Canyon Country, 18
United States Geological Survey, 9, 11
Unkakaniguts, juniper shelters of the, *63*
Upper Granite Gorge, *88*
Utah Lake, 16, 17
Ute Creek, 99 n.

Vasey's Paradise, Marble Canyon, *51*, 102
Vermilion Cliffs, 16, 107
Vermilion River, 41
Virgin River, 9, 14, 18, 97, 142, 145

Wasatch Mountains, 49, 55, 58, 67, 97
Wasatch Plateau, 16, 17
Waterpocket Fold, 23
Wheeler, Lieutenant George, 9
Whirlpool Canyon, 57, 58
White, James, rafting in Grand Canyon, 14
White Canyon, 152
White River, 58
Whitmore Wash, columnar basalt at, *140*
Wilson Canyon, *12*
Wind River Mountains, 55
Wyoming Territory, 9

Yampa River, and Green River, 52–56
Young, Brigham, 9, 20